BIRDS

of the

Lake District

Common Wren

By the same author:

A FEW MILLION BIRDS
BIRDWATCH ROUND SCOTLAND
HIGHLAND SPRING
WEST HIGHLAND SUMMER
HIGHLAND AUTUMN
HIGHLAND WINTER
A YEAR WITH THE CURLEWS
PENNINE BIRDS (with Bill Robson)
LAKELAND BIRDS (with Bill Robson)
BIRD-WATCHING IN YORKSHIRE (with Bob Dickens)
A PASSION FOR PUFFINS (illustrated by David Binns)
*BIRDS OF THE YORKSHIRE DALES (illustrated by David Binns)

* *This title is still in print*

BIRDS

of the

Lake District

by

W R Mitchell

MBE, Hon D.Litt.

Illustrated

by

David Binns

Two voices there are, one is of the Sea,
One of the mountains, each a mighty voice.

William Wordsworth

CASTLEBERG

2000

The Author

Bill Mitchell's fascination with Lakeland bird-life began half a century ago and expressed itself through membership of the RSPB and of the Committee at the Hay Bridge Nature Reserve in Southern Lakeland when the little estate was owned by Tissie Fooks. He has served on the committee of the North West branch of the British Deer Society and is a member of the Cumbrian Wildlife Trust. For almost 40 years he edited the magazine *Cumbria*. He was the joint author with Bill Robson of the book "Lakeland Birds," published in 1974. "Birds of the Lake Counties" is a companion of the author's "Birds of the Yorkshire Dales."

The Artist

David Binns, a north-country bird artist of distinction, has examples of his water-colours in many private collections. He exhibits at the annual exhibition of Wildlife Artists and has received special awards from the Royal Society for the Protection of Birds. David illustrated the aforementioned "Birds of the Yorkshire Dales."

A **Castleberg** Book.
First published in the United Kingdom in 2000.

ISBN 1 871064 64 3
Typeset in Palatino, printed and bound in the United Kingdom by
Lamberts Print & Design, Station Road, Settle, North Yorkshire, BD24 9AA.
Published by Castleberg, 18 Yealand Avenue, Giggleswick, Settle, North Yorkshire, BD24 0AY.

Contents

Our cover picture is of a golden eagle.
Maps by Christine Denmead.
The illustrations were prepared using the scraperboard process. David Binns used the white variety and the picture of Friars Crag, by his late father, Dan, was on the black variety.

Lakeland Habitat:
Friars Crag, Derwentwater
A scraperboard by Dan Binns

Foreword

by Peter Bullard

Director, Cumbria Wildlife Trust

THE LAKE DISTRICT is one of the most renowned and popular of all the National Parks and birds are the most popular part of our Natural World. Surprisingly the Lake District is not immediately associated as a major bird watching destination; the lakes and mountains are the first attraction in most people's hearts and minds.

This book is therefore perfect for those who love birds and visit the Lake District or those who love the Lake District and want to discover more about its birds. This is far more than a book about what birds there are and where you might find them. A hundred and one bird books do that already, and this is a companion to those books – a book about the birds themselves and the people associated with them.

As Director of Cumbria Wildlife Trust, most of my work and the work of the Trust is to do with conserving Wildlife in Cumbria, which of course includes birds. Books like *Birds of the Lake District* are particularly welcome as they both inform, educate and enthuse people about the wildlife that surrounds them. If everyone was as knowledgeable, interested and enthusiastic about wildlife as Bill Mitchell we wouldn't need any Wildlife Charities. Through his books, therefore, Bill makes a major contribution to nature conservation.

The Lake District is a wonderful place to enjoy birds, as this book testifies. However, the Lake District continues to suffer desperately from the overgrazing of sheep which drastically reduces the population of many birds. The agricultural support system is changing slowly but surely away from production subsidies to environmental payments. Hopefully, as we end one Millennium and start another, the bird life of the Lake District will get better and better. This book will help in that process.

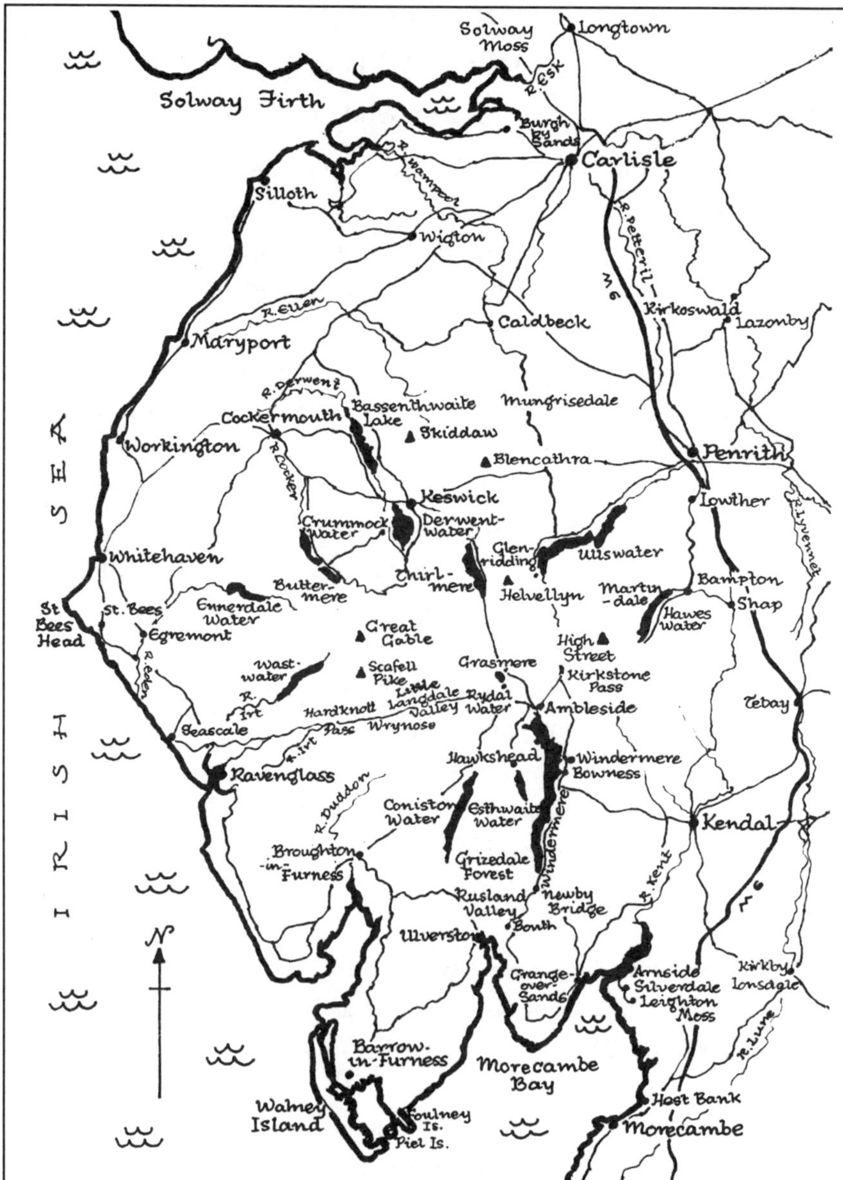

Some Topographical Features of the Lake District and its Environs

Introduction

Birds of the Lake District is for those who know a little about birds – but would like to know more. The bird species selected are those typical of north-west England – its mountains, dales, woods, estuaries and coastline. Take pleasure not only in the birds but also in their wild settings.

This book takes in the high fells where the ravens play hide-and-seek in mist and will greet you with husky voices. The reader will be encouraged to visit old woodland where jays chatter and pied flycatchers flick their wings and utter thin, scrapy songs. The new conifer plantations, such as those on Claife Heights, west of Windermere, will offer sightings of redpoll, siskin and the crossbill, a bird that is brown and brick-red, with a top-heavy appearance and twisted mandibles that deftly remove seeds from cones. On the shores of the quieter lakes, listen to the cheery call of the sandpiper, a summer visitor known to the Lakers of old as Willie Liltie. In spring, while standing by a reed-bed at Leighton Moss, you might mistake the "boom" of one of the local bitterns for a foghorn at nearby Morecambe Bay.

At the seabird city of St Bees are growling guillemots and laughing gulls. At South Walney, follow paths between massed ranks of gulls and see eiders squatting on their nests, which they have lagged with down plucked from their bodies. A sitting eider looks for all the world like a feathered tea-cosy. The first eiders bred on Walney in 1941, since when there has developed a large colony, the most southerly on the west coast of Britain. At Drigg and Walney, our understanding of the gull colonies owes much to the research conducted in the 1960s by Professor Niko Tinbergen and the Animal Behaviour Department of Oxford University.

Birds of the Lake District might be used in conjunction with a bird identification book in which the species are shown in glowing colours, though a free-ranging bird rarely stays around long enough to have its plumage studied. The dashing peregrine, so bright on a picture, may in reality be nothing more than a silhouette against a scudding cloud. Consider, in the fleeting moments before a bird takes flight, its size, manner and voice.

Brief notes stress the points of special interest and are followed by more detailed information, with the emphasis throughout on Lakeland. The sketches of David Binns are of special value, having been based on studies in the wild. A brief account of local geology and a short historical review of bird associations with the Lake District will provide background material for the bird-watching pleasures to come.

Vernacular names of Lakeland birds are used where known, though anomalies are to be found. For example, to the folk of Bewcastle, in northern Cumbria, the hedge sparrow (now more widely known as the dunnock) was Hemplin. And this name was used in West Cumberland for the linnet, which bird-fanciers were inclined to call "whin-grey."

A range of Lakeland bird haunts is presented with simple maps. An orderly list of birds, forming the final section, will appeal to those who like to tick off any species they have seen. Little space has been devoted to descriptions of nests and eggs. It is illegal to interfere with them. Rejoice in the living bird.

The Lakeland bird-watcher needs a good pair of binoculars, though do not be tempted by those that are impressively large. Binoculars with a magnification of between 7 and 10 should give a reasonably large image and also be capable of being focussed on objects near at hand. Needless to say, binoculars should be light enough to be held without undue fatigue.

Bird-watching maintains its appeal for many because of changes in the landscape and in the status of individual species. The bird population of the Lake District is currently in a period of rapid change. The red-breasted merganser made its first appearance as a breeding species in the early 1950s, when nesting took place in the sand dunes near Ravenglass. The collared dove has spread remarkably since its debut in the 1970s. The corncrake, which kept our ancestors awake during summer nights by its calling, is no longer counted among the breeding birds and with the drainage and re-seeding of many fields the number of nesting waders has declined. And so has the once-great moulting flock of curlew in the Eden Valley.

Nuthatches have an assured food supply in winter in the well-stocked bird table. Great spotted woodpeckers hack their way into bird boxes put out for titmice. Cormorants, which once were thought of as coastal birds, now pursue perch – and sometimes char – in Windermere and may be seen on virtually every other lake. Reed warblers, here at the northern part of their breeding range, and other species, are likely to extend the range even further north through global warming. With maturing plantations there has been a northward spread of lesser spotted woodpeckers.

At one time, the nesting season was the main time for bird study. Now many bird-watchers keenly anticipate the migrations of spring and autumn and the bustle among wintering birds. Then the sky above the Solway is patterned by the lines and chevrons of grey geese. To the south, knot and dunlin form dense packs along the line of the ebb tide in Morecambe Bay.

Rev Hugh Alexander Macpherson, author of *The Vertebrate Fauna of Lakeland* (1892), provided us with a most valuable historical work on the region's bird life. Macpherson, who was appointed curate of St Cuthbert's Church, Carlisle, in 1882, became a zoologist of international repute. Like William Wordsworth – poet, naturalist and conservationist – he made an effort to convey the manner as well as the appearance of common birds.

Macpherson's ring ouzel had "a cheery presence" and the wheatear, another springtime visitor, was "a bright, joyous bird, at one moment carolling blithely on the wing with fond half-hovering flight, and the next balancing its slight form on some conspicuous vantage point..." The cleric wrote of wintering redwings that were "aimlessly drifting about the fields as if at a loss to find shelter from the showers of driving sleet."

When I took up bird-watching in Lakeland, I could consult men who remembered the Victorian period. Joe Farren, of Ravenglass, had rowed visiting naturalists across the estuary to visit the gulls and terns of Drigg Point. One of his passengers had been Richard Kearton, a pioneer of bird photography, complete with bulky camera, tripod and stack of sensitive plates. Among my mentors was Ernest Blezard, who had become keeper of natural history at Tullie House Museum in Carlisle in 1926. Ernest, a first-rate field naturalist, made springtime jaunts to observe the nesting of ravens and one winter was taken aloft by a friend who owned a light aircraft and, for a while, they flew with the grey geese of his beloved Solway.

Bill Robson of New Hall, near Appleby, was among a dedicated group of bird-ringers, his special interest being with the birds of the high Pennines. On the dunes of South Walney, I met Walter the warden, whose old felt hat was plastered with white when irate gulls defended their new-hatched chicks. At Walney and also at Ravenglass, it was stimulating to chat with the biologist Niko Tinbergen who, when most scientists were inclined to work in stuffy laboratories, opened a window and let in a blast of fresh air. He conducted some outstanding field studies on the Cumbrian coast.

Another ornithologist of note at the time when my bird-watching began was J A G Barnes, whose private school overlooked the bird-busy Kent Estuary. He wrote a monograph on the titmouse family and was joint editor and contributor of the section on birds to *Natural History of the Lake District*, published in 1970. He was conscious that although the avifauna of the Lake District is not as rich as that of some parts of southern England, it does include birds of particular interest and beauty that cannot be found in lowland districts. The central fells offered him and other bird-watchers a chance to study familiar birds like the chaffinch, wren and dunnock as high-level species.

In the company of Stan Lythe, a bird photographer, I was able to have close views of familiar Pennine birds. Stan, who invariably kept "unsocial hours," was also fond of the woods of South Lakeland, especially a tract near Whitbarrow where he watched the mysterious nightjars, summer visitors who plucked from the sky a variety of moths and beetles.

During the day the birds rested on the ground , their streaky-brown plumage providing excellent camouflage. At dusk, they took flight, mouths agape, wheeling and zigzagging, trawling for food. On bright nights, it was possible to see white spots on wings and tail. The night air seemed to shiver as a nightjar clapped its wings and vibrated when a male bird, having settled lengthways along a tree branch, rendered a churring song. One observer has compared the sound with "a badly-tuned, two-stroke engine."

Tufted duck

Lakeland: An Overview

The Lake District may be small by Scottish or Continental standards but it is compact and wondrously varied – 866 square miles of fells, dales and lakes, with the National Park as its core. The highest hills exceed 2,500ft/750m. The fells are relatively bare, with scree slopes and dark crags. Lakes occupy many of the deep valleys.

The border of the Park meanders between Caldbeck, "back o' Skiddaw," and the estuaries flowing into Morecambe Bay; and from Ravenglass to the M6. Norman Nicholson wrote a book about the peripheral areas under the title *Greater Lakeland*. Considering the whole county, I conclude that it is virtually an island, washed in the west by the Irish Sea and in the north and south by the tides that sweep into Solway Firth and Morecambe Bay.

The coastline is generally low, consisting of dunes and tidal flats. The exceptions are Humphrey Head, a limestone hump by the sea, and the spectacular outcrop of New Red Sandstone at St Bees, the resort of sea birds, including the only black guillemots in England.

To the east, the island "feel" is imparted by six lanes of the M.6 which cuts through the upper Lune Valley, over Shap and into the Eden Valley, spanning the gap between the great sea inlets of Morecambe and Solway and inhibiting the movement of terrestrial mammals though not, of course, of birds, which are unaware of man-made boundaries. The county of Cumbria came into being in 1974, combining Cumberland, Westmorland, Lancashire North of the Sands – the old divisions of the north-west – with the whole of the Howgills, those rounded Silurian fells, most of which were traditionally in the West Riding of Yorkshire.

Lake District is an off-comer's term, as indeed is the word mountain. The old-time Norse settlers called it a "fell." The name Cumbrian Hills is printed in large letters across older maps of Lakeland. There is said to be only one lake in the region, this being Bassenthwaite Lake in the north. Most large stretches of water have as a suffix either "mere" or "water" – watter, if you are native born. Norse settlers bestowed the term "dale" on the valleys that radiate from the central hub of high fells.

Many of the dales contain lakes that range in size from Windermere, England's largest at 10 miles, to Rydal Water, at the heart of Wordsworthshire, an unofficial name derived from that of a former distinguished resident. Lakeland artist Heaton Cooper described the upland tarns as "the eyes of the mountains."

Dozens of fells, the haunt of ravens, extend to over 2,000 ft. Four summits overtop 3,000 ft, and Scafell Pike is, at 3,210 ft, the highest point in England. Birds are thinly spread on the slate and volcanic rock that give the Lake District its acidic character. The corries are echo-chambers for the fluty calls of ring ouzels, the white-bibbed mountain blackbirds. Other high-fell sounds are the croak of a raven and the stuttering cry – *kee, kee, kee, kee* – of the peregrine, our "great blue hawk." The peregrines used to leave their craggy haunts to winter in the low country. Now, when there are generally mild winters, some of them tend to remain in Lakeland the year through, to the detriment of the ravens who, nesting early in the year, were previously able to occupy their favourite sites. Some of these were now the eyries of falcons.

Names on the map hint at the old-time avifauna. Eagle Crag, Glead Howe ("hill of the kite"), Falcon Crag and several Raven Crags give a romantic touch to the locality. All the birds mentioned except the red kite still nest here and, red kites having been released in neighbouring Yorkshire, it is surely just a matter of time before they extend their range to the Lake District. The golden eagle has a tenuous hold on the region and the dotterel is decidedly rare.

Goosander and red-breasted merganser – known as sawbills because of the serrated edges to their bills – are regular nesters. In 1885, the merganser was being described as "essentially a marine species." The Wildlife and Countryside Act (1981) allows both goosanders and red-breasted mergansers to be legally shot if a licence has been printed by the Ministry of Agriculture, Fisheries and Food. For a licence to be granted, it has to be decided that the birds are inflicting serious damage to fisheries, although undoubtedly many are also shot illegally. Unfortunately, no one has yet defined what amounts of "serious damage." This ambiguous statement has led to clashes between bird-watchers and anglers.

The "western oakwoods," of the type which Coast to Coast walkers see as they trudge along the path by Loweswater, are lagged with mosses, liverworts and ferns and sustain a diversity of bird life, buzzards to wood warblers. Elsewhere, coppice woods were clear-felled every 17 years or so to sustain a variety of woodland crafts. The old crafts have gone and the coppice woods have developed into mature woodland. Trees past their best offer nesting holes for pied flycatchers and are used as "sounding boards" by great spotted woodpeckers. The yaffle [laughing cry] of the green woodpecker is heard in spring. Crossbill and siskin are at home in tracts of conifers.

Waterfowl have wintering quarters in lakes with shallow bays, an example being Windermere, where is to be found some 5% of the European population of goldeneye. After many years as a wildfowler, Jim Ellwood of Millom opened a bird reserve at The Hawes, near the Duddon Estuary, and by hatching out eggs from Scottish greylags and giving the hatched geese their freedom, re-established the ancestor of the domestic goose as a Cumbrian-nesting species. Grey geese from this source are nesting widely. In late autumn, they are joined in the Eden Valley by skeins of Iceland-nesting birds.

The most glamorous of the nesting birds is the pair of golden eagles that nest on a crag above Riggindale and may be watched from an RSPB hide set up in the little valley. The first native-hatched eaglet flew safely from the eyrie on 28 July, 1970. The Nature Conservancy and the Royal Society for the Protection of Birds had organised a full-time watch over the nest and made the historic event possible.

In recent years, the lordly eagles have rarely brought off young. Are the birds past their reproductive best? A shiver of excitement passed through the Lakeland naturalist fraternity when eagles returned after an absence of almost 200 years. The return had been confidently forecast by Ernest Blezard. He had been told that a pair of eagles was nesting just north of Solway, within easy viewing range of our northern fells.

Conservation of wildlife is undertaken by The National Trust, one of the major Lakeland landowners, with about 140,000 acres/56,655 ha. Many Sites of Special Scientific Interest are to be found on Trust properties. Special protection has been given to woodland, including the old deciduous woods on the limestone beside Morecambe Bay. North-West Water, with about 38,500 acres/15,560 ha., includes in the large catchment areas associated with reservoirs. It has taken practical steps to cater for the welfare of wildlife.

The Cumbria Wildlife Trust, formed as the Lake District Naturalists' Trust in 1962, manages 40 nature reserves, advises on conservation issues and carries out research into aspects of Lakeland fauna and flora. The Trust, which is essentially a voluntary organisation, is directly concerned with wildlife on a total acreage of 4,500. The Forestry Commission is transforming, through mixed planting, what were once monotonous blocks of conifer trees. In the Lake District, its flagship venture is at Grizedale Forest, near Hawkshead.

Back to Basics

Geology

Over 300 million years have elapsed since the oldest rocks in the Lake District were folded and tilted. The final uplift, which took place around 50 million years ago, created a dome, which explains why the drainage is roughly radial around the central massif. Wordsworth was one of those who first compared this with a wheel.

Lakeland geology is complex but generally there are three major zones of visible rocks that lie in belts from ENE to WSW. Their names are Skiddaw Slates, Borrowdale Volcanics and Silurian. Almost ringing the Lake District is Carboniferous Limestone, a sedimentary rock formed in a clear, shallow sea, largely from the shells of marine creatures. The New Red Sandstone, seen outstandingly in the Eden Valley, at St Bees and at Furness Abbey, near modern Barrow, was laid down in arid conditions.

Skiddaw Slates, of Ordovician age, are the oldest visible rocks. They are named after the fell of that name in the northern area and are a mixture of generally dark strata – of grits, flags, shales and mudstones, deposited in an ancient sea about 450 million years ago. The slates are believed to have a thickness of some 6,000 ft. These Slates are soft, eroding easily and evenly. Apart from Skiddaw, the typical long, smooth slope occurs on Grisedale Pike, Mellbreak and Grasmoor. An isolated outcrop of the Slates is to be seen at Black Combe, above the Duddon, in the south-west.

Borrowdale Volcanics are represented by fells that are steep, high-soaring, craggy and bleak. Here is a mixture of lavas and ashes that accumulated to a thickness of from 8,000 to 12,000 ft. At Honister Pass, between Borrowdale and Buttermere, the Slates and Volcanic rocks are cheek-by-jowl, with the Slates to the left of the road (notice heaps of discarded slate from quarries) and the Volcanic rocks on the right.

Canon G A K Hervey, writing about Helvellyn in 1960, considered the principal bird of these volcanic crags was the raven. Buzzards kept mostly to the lower slopes. Ring ouzels frequented the rocky streams. Wheatears and meadow pipits were abundant below the crags "and the great charm of the woodlands is the number of pied flycatchers to be seen and heard."

The Volcanic Series was overlaid, unconformably, by Coniston Limestone, which is represented on the surface by a narrow band composed of volcanic material and muddy limestones stretching south-westwards from Shap to Millom.

Silurian rocks, to the south of the Volcanics, were formed of sediments that settled in estuarial conditions and are made up of mudstones, grits, flagstones and shales. They give the landscape a rolling appearance. The distinctive crags and hollows are seen to the best effect around Windermere and Esthwaite Water.

Carboniferous Limestone almost encircles the Lake District. In the east, there is an upward sweep of ground to the Pennine plateau, a succession of treeless solitudes forming a nesting ground for upland waders like the golden plover, curlew and dunlin. The short-eared owl, which hunts by day, flits across the ground like a big brown moth.

Vegetation

Note the large expanses of flat ground at the head of such valleys as Great Langdale and Buttermere. The alluvium soil has been washed down from the fells. The rocky fell tops have a vegetation similar to that in the sub-arctic because of the severe climate at high elevations. A restricted flora of higher plants is present with an abundant cover of mosses and lichens. The majority of plants above the tree-line are widespread elsewhere in moorland situations in Britain.

Since the Ice Age, vegetation on the fells has been modified and impoverished by man. Early Man cleared areas of native forest. Norse settlers made a considerable impact, judging by the number of place-names with thwaite as a suffix, for this was a Norse term for "clearing." In the upper dales, a considerable amount of rock debris must have been cleared at Stonethwaite in Borrowdale.

Much of the cleared material found its way into drystone walls to divide up the land and restrain any stock. At the head of Wasdale, spare stone is seen in neat heaps as part of a web-like pattern of walls, in some of which birds like the pied wagtail find secure nesting places. The grazing of sheep, which was heavy from monastic times, checked the natural regeneration of the forest. Much native woodland was coppice for the production of charcoal needed to smelt the locally-mined iron ore.

Drier ridges on the Lakeland fells support grassland, with sheep's fescue as a valuable species. Bracken has become common, spreading into erstwhile pastures because the husbandry practised on hill farms is less intense than it was. Bracken cannot stand trampling by domestic stock – or, indeed, the boots of the many ramblers. Over-grazing by sheep during the 1939-45 war was the beginning of a process that has modified the grazing on many fells and has led to the invasion of unpalatable mat-grass.

Heather is locally common, the most notable tract of moorland being on Skiddaw Forest and the ridges of Blencathra. In wet areas, the flowering heads of cotton-grass (a sedge) are to be seen. This was one of the great peat-forming plants.

Of the trees, a few rowan and birch trees endure conditions at up to 1,900 ft, but the tree-line is at about 1,500 ft. High-lying oakwoods, relics of the old climax vegetation, are seen at Keskadale and Rigg Beck, in Newlands Valley, and at Naddle beside Haweswater. Extensive woodland on the lower fells and the sides of dales contain native species – oak, ash, birch and hazel. Alder, which borders many streams, is attractive to finches, particularly siskin and redpoll. The yew has long thrived in Lakeland judging by such placenames as

Yewdale, Yew Crags, Yew Pike and Yew Tree Tarn.

Since the 18th century, Lakeland has become host to introduced conifers. An early introduction was European larch. William Wordsworth, beholding the new larch plantations at a time when the northern cities were being transformed by the Industrial Revolution, described them as "vegetable manufactury."

Exotics were also being planted in the extensive grounds of houses built by wealthy folk who, using the new-fangled railway as a form of transport, were settling along the shore of Windermere. They had a fondness for rhododendron, which soon was smothering the chosen tracts of ground. John Marshall, a Leeds flax manufacturer, created Tarn Hows near Coniston by damming up an area where hitherto were several small tarns. Lebanese cedar and Norway spruce no longer look strange at this picturesque spot.

Fen, carr and bog at low elevation are prime bird haunts. Such habitats are found by Bassenthwaite and Esthwaite Water.

Climate

John Gough, a 19th century bird-watcher living at Kendal, related his observations closely to the weather. He wrote: "The cuckoo arrives in Westmorland about the end of April, when the mean temperature is 49 deg and the noon-tide heat frequently higher than 60 deg. This seems to indicate that a considerable degree of temperature is necessary to this bird, but I heard one crying merrily on the evening of the 23rd of May, 1814, when the thermometer stood at 41 deg: the hills were covered with snow and the wind blew strong from the north-east."

The Lakeland climate is varied but is generally wet and cloudy, as befits a mountainous area beside the sea. Summers are not very hot, nor winters – apart from on the high fells – bitterly cold. The region is drier and sunnier than cynics like to imagine, thought it depends on where you go. In the central fells area, less than 1,000 hours of sunshine are annually recorded. The average annual rainfall in central Lakeland is around 60 inches/150mm.

Lakeland has no permanent snow cover. Snow lies on summits over 2,500 feet on about 100 days a year. The first falls can occur in September and the last in May, even June. The cores of ancient drifts may be found in northern gullies on Midsummer Day.

The prevailing winds are westerly. Gusts of wind in Wasdale have been known to whisk water from the lake and deposit it on the Screes up to 200 ft. Yachtsmen on Windermere comment on the way the flanking hills break up an air flow so that in places gusts might reach them from several directions simultaneously. Honister Crag, above Buttermere, is where an air flow divided by fells is reunited with an awesome sound and savage effect. It is known as "t'wind in the crack."

Lakeland rainfall totals decline from south-west to north-east. Fell-tops have a much higher rainfall than do the dales. On the coastal region, an annual fall of about 44 inches might be compared with the 150 to 200 inches recorded in fell-country less than 20 miles away. The average annual at the well-named Sprinkling Tarn, beneath Great End, is about 185 inches.

The Borrowdale rainfall figures fall off dramatically in a few miles. Styhead on the fells has 170 inches. Seathwaite, at the head of its own little valley, the topmost part of Borrowdale, is reputed to be the wettest inhabited spot in England with 131 inches. Rosthwaite (lower down the valley) expects just over 100 inches and Grange (by the Jaws of Borrowdale) about 90. Yet Keswick and Cockermouth record 58 inches and rather more than 40 inches respectively.

At Coniston, the average rainfall is over 75 inches and Kendal's is about 50 inches. Springtime droughts have been experienced in recent times.

Wings Over Lakeland

Snow Buntings

For about 600,000 years, what is now the Lake District was a playground of glaciers. "Rivers of ice" modified the landscape. Their abrasive action widened and deepened the old river valleys, plucked out corries and, having collected rock debris from a freeze-thaw process on the crags, scooped out basins that would become lakes. The bed of Wastwater, our deepest lake, lies below sea-level. Blea Water, the deepest tarn, occupies a "pocket" of the fell-country to the south of Haweswater.

The latest of several periods of glaciation was probably confined to the high fells. As the climate ameliorated, birds and beasts found the conditions tolerable. It is tempting to think of snowy owls moving like big white moths across tundral areas and of snow buntings fluttering, with jingling calls, across the austere landscape.

There would be a time when ptarmigan scuttered among the lichened rocks of high places, communicating with croaky voices and matching their plumage to changing surroundings by the ploy of having three moults a year. Melting ice led to rising sea levels. Some 6,000 years ago, the low country separating what is now Britain from the Continent was flooded. A bird species now known as red grouse became an island form of the widespread Arctic willow grouse, a white-winged species. In more moderate conditions, the red grouse retained its dark plumage and, indeed, both sexes turned darker in winter, though the cock birds retained white-feathered legs and feet.

In the Lakeland of long ago, the gruff voices of ravens would break

Bittern

the stillness of the high fells as they do to this day. From the lakes, in spring, came the wail of divers. Whooper swans would rear their grey downy young beside standing water. On the shores of Solway Firth and Morecambe Bay, where (wrote a Victorian writer) there lay "extensive morasses...and quaking bogs," the low-pitched "boom" of a lovelorn bittern might be heard. The bittern, with its cryptic "burnt toast" plumage of brown, buff and black, is still to be found at Leighton Moss, to the south of Lakeland.

The Rev H A Macpherson described the "quaking bogs" as places that "defied the most adventurous spirits to traverse on foot their treacherous surface." At Drumburgh, in 1610, the bittern was known as *myre drumble* "because she haunteth myres, boggs, fens and carrs, and for that she had a thundering voice which we call rumbling." At about the same time, by Morecambe Bay a parson was stalking homeward "with nought in view but dreary dykes and dusky ling" when he was startled by the cries of *herrensue* [heron] and *miredrum* [bittern].

Harking back to ancient time, the bird life of Lakeland became much more varied with the spread of trees. The tenacious but short-lived birch was a pioneering species, just as today it clothes the heaps of debris left over by slate-quarrying. After birch came pine and then the climax was reached with oak woodland, the resort of many of the birds with which we are familiar today.

In the early Middle Ages, when much of the land was unkempt, and there were tracts of scrub, moor and bog, black grouse converged on leks, their assembly places where cock birds displayed and hen birds (known as greyhens) assessed the finest of the stock before moving in to be mated. Placenames like Cocklaw perpetuate the old time association of bird and mating-ground. The pounding feet of blackcock, described by a Lakeland gamekeeper as "big as a littleish turkey," crushed the vegetation to something with the appearance of coconut matting. Reacting to a diurnal clock, the cock birds kept their dawn appointment at a time which varied only by minutes as the days lengthened. They pranced with inflated wattles, drooping wings and under-tail coverts fanned out to provide patches of gleaming whiteness. Their curious vocabulary consisted of dove-like cooing, of bubbling calls and explosive hisses.

The capercaillie that would inhabit the pinewoods during the long dry period that preceded one of extreme wetness attracted females by a curious vocal medley consisting of a tapping and a popping and a gurgling. It was from Scotland, in the spring of 1968, that "caper" eggs were transported some 300 miles to Grizedale Forest, in Lakeland, where efforts were made to hatch them out in the hope the young birds could be released into the wild. Colonies of wood ants, necessary to the welfare of young caper, were introduced into Grizedale, but the scheme did not succeed. One reason was that the caper chicks, when quite young, were inclined to damage themselves, in a bid for freedom, by dashing against the wire that surrounded their enclosures. The intention had been to release them when they were much older. The capercaillie, largest grouse in the world, also doubtless found the Lake District too wet for its comfort.

An early reference to the peregrine, the "big blue hawk," occurred in a tribute of Middleton, Lunesdale, during the 13th century, when annually a "cast" of peregrines were removed from an eyrie in nearby Barbondale and presented to the overlord. Falconry was not just a sport; it was also a means of collecting birds with a food value. Falconers had their own strange language in which a nestling was known as an eyass until, at the age of two or three weeks, it became a *ramage hawk*, then a *brancher*, graduating to a *soar-hawk* when fledged.

Good to Eat

To the cartographer Speed, who visited Cumberland in 1611, this part of England was "overspread with a great variety of fowls." Norman lords and their favourites indulged their love of hunting in the *foris*, a tract of land set apart for hunting. In such an area, special laws protected the game and so a tract like Inglewood, in the Eden Valley between Penrith and Carlisle, was in effect a nature reserve.

The birds about which most is known were those that were shot, firstly for sport and secondly for the table. Certain birds provided tasty additions to the diet, especially in winter, when most people subsisted for months on meat that had been salted down, if they had meat at all. The pigeon-cote was such a source of fresh meat. The great families who lived at the periphery of Lakeland but had vast estates kept game books in which were entered details of what had been slain. The main items were deer. A red deer represented some 300 lb of venison.

The accounts kept by the household of Lord William Howard of Naworth in 1620 mentions the fieldfare, the name being written as "felde fare." The song thrush was listed as "thossel." Each was valued at a penny. In 1621 is mention of "a pig, a capon and young starlins, ij s. iij d." One proud family in Edendale had on their coat of arms "three black cocks [the male of the black grouse species]" and a crossbow was pictured between them. At the aforementioned Naworth, the stately castle of the Howards, east of Carlisle, the accounts of Lord William between August and December, 1618, recorded bags of 120 black grouse and 145 red grouse. At that time, a *Black Cock* cost 6d, a *Grey Hen* [female of the species] was 4d. The red grouse was worth threepence.

If a shortage of a toothsome species occurred in one area, a fresh stock might be introduced from another. This occurred in the Rusland Valley between 1832 and 1840. A writer in the *Westmorland Gazette* in September, 1845, lamented the decline of the black grouse, which were absent from the "high hills of Westmorland and Cumberland." By this time, guns were available to those whose pleasure was the pursuit of wild creatures.

Efforts to re-introduce black grouse were not as successful as the landowner hoped. "Mr B Hawkrigg, of Sawrey, shot four of these rare birds on the hills between Windermere and Esthwaite which are supposed to have been bred in the plantations of H Curwen, Esq; but how they came to take up their abode in this locality must remain a mystery. We understand that there are four of the brood still left, and that strict orders have been given for their preservation."

In the mid-19th century, black grouse were to be found between Crook and Underbarrow and in the extensive larch woods at Lamb How in Crosthwaite. They also occurred on the summit of Whitbarrow, "a detached limestone mountain, presenting a grand rock escarpment to the lake tourist, as he approaches from Milnthorpe." They occurred in the [mixed coppice] woods of Furness Fells, on the western side of the lake [Windermere] and were also to be seen "as far down...as Holker Hall."

Red grouse from the moors of North Cumberland were despatched to the Antipodes. John Boustead, of Armathwaite Hall, sent five brace to New Zealand in 1870. Unfortunately only one bird reached its destination alive. "Far from being discouraged by this misadventure, Mr Boustead had eleven and a-half brace of birds taken from Binsey [near the outflow of Bassenthwaite Lake] and reared by hand, in 1872. This installment was shipped for the Colony in November of the same year."

In the early 17th century we have records of cranes and herons being among the birds consumed at Cumbrian banquets. At Naworth, the Howards dined on wolde-gouse [wild goose]. One snag about shooting free-ranging geese was an inability to assess their age by appearances. A goose was a long-lived bird and the flesh of the oldest of them was only just chewable.

Of the grey geese, the bean goose was once the most common visitor. Most of the birds seen in or along the coast of Cumbria were in passage from their European nesting grounds to winter quarters in Ireland. A writer living by Solway Firth noted: "As a rule they are very wary. They scarcely ever allow a punt to work up to them, and are chiefly shot when they are feeding in the evening or early morning." Pink-footed geese were much less common than they are today. In the Victorian period, both dark and light-breasted brent geese occurred on the estuaries of Cumbria.

The swan, elaborately dressed, was to be found on the tables of the well-to-do on festive occasions. At Christmastide, 1661, Sir Daniel Fleming bought a swan for one shilling and it was greatly enjoyed by him and his family at their home at Rydal.

Birds as "Vermin"

The records of Lakeland churchwardens include references to bounty money paid to those who slew bird pests. Farmers and shepherds living in the upper dales of the Lake District waged war against birds with hooked beaks with such gusto that, by the end of the 18th century, raptors were uncommon. In a relatively few years, Lakeland lost its once spectacular avifauna, which had consisted of golden eagle, sea eagle, three species of harriers, goshawk, kite, hobby, osprey and three species of buzzard.

Church records give us a stark review of the campaign against ravens. Derek Ratcliffe, in his monograph *The Raven* (1997), reports that the earliest church records were for the parish of Orton, Westmorland, in 1636-37, when the price per head was a penny. By 1649, the price for adult birds had doubled though that for young birds remained at a penny. The first Hawkshead records (1731) mention that fourpence was paid for each of four ravens. The figure was unchanged for half a century.

Cartmel Priory paid only twopence by an order decreed in 1751. Ratcliffe found the longest run of records associated with Greystoke parish. Over a 90-year period, between 1752 and 1842, the churchwardens accounted for 966 raven payments.

The demise of the golden and sea eagles as nesting species was hastened by headage payments. An early reference to eagles appears in a document written between 1272 and 1307 about Nichol Forest district in Cumberland, when the accent was on preservation. Part of the forest was let "and they of the forest [the small tenants] must preserve the nests of sparrow hawks and eagles." Confusion has existed in Lakeland between the golden eagle and its cousin the sea (or white-tailed) eagle, which was also known as the erne. (Hence the several Heron Crags and Pikes which were indeed used by eagles).

A pair of white-tails were the last of the eagle tribe to lay eggs in Lakeland until the return of golden eagles in recent times. According to James Clark (1787) white-tails nested on Wallow Crag, near Haweswater, in 1787, assembling in the eyrie 35 fish, "besides 7 lambs and other provisions for the young one." A pair was seen in Eskdale in the 1780s. A shepherd on Black Combe captured a bird in 1838.

It is reported that a pair of eagles once nested on Blea Crag, Grasmere. You will find Eagle Crags, the name almost certainly referring to golden eagles, at the junction of the Langstrath and Greenup Valleys off Borrowdale, in Easedale, Ennerdale, Grizedale and Riggindale. The golden eagle is known to have nested on Burtness Combe in Buttermere, on Buck Crag, Martindale and in Patterdale.

In Borrowdale, a rope was kept so that intrepid young men might be lowered down a crag to an eyrie. Not only was there a bounty to be earned but both eggs and fledglings commanded a good price from collectors. The Borrowdale eagle rope, "long and strong," was also available for Buttermere, Langdale, Eskdale and other valleys. The Crosthwaite (Keswick) records show that in 1713 John Jackson received a shilling for slaying an old eagle and Edward Berket received sixpence "for a young eagle." These records indicate that more than 30 eagles were killed between 1713 and 1765, the birds being counted as vermin, along with foxes, ravens and polecats.

Eagles last nested in Borrowdale in about 1765. Green, in his *New Guide* (1819) mentioned that John Vicars of Gatesgarth twice robbed the nest of its young. The Rev W Richardson noted that the golden eagle nested in Martindale in 1787 and 1789. "The first year the female was shot, and the male after an absence of about three weeks returned with another female. The next year, 1789, the male was killed after which the female disappeared." The last golden eagle to be shot in Lakeland fell to the gun of Farmer Jenkinson of Dunnerdale about 1860. The late Ernest Blezard heard the story of Jenkinson's adventure from descendants of the farmer.

Jenkinson carried his muzzle-loader on his rounds and had one or two unsuccessful shots at an eagle. Then, concealing himself and ramming a "turrible gurt charge" of powder and lead down his weapon, he lay flat on his back in the heather. When the eagle passed over, he fired vertically, winged the bird and himself sustained a broken collarbone from the violent recoil of a gun checked by the unyielding ground. The eagle fell into a bobbin mill dam and "gave further account of itself before it was despatched and carried home to Hole House Farm, where its full-spread wings were found almost to span the small kitchen."

For almost 200 years, the golden eagle was classified as a rare vagrant. Then, in 1957, an adult bird was seen flying near a Lakeland crag on which a newly-built nest was found. A three-year-old female eagle, found lying dead in Bretherdale, near Shap, in December, 1960, had one leg fastened in a rabbit trap, which it had possibly carried for miles. The first golden eagle eggs to be laid on a Lakeland crag for about 160 years were seen in an eyrie in March 1969. The eggs failed to hatch and in 1971 the nesting site was forsaken for a new eyrie a little distance away. Here a singleton was reared. The site, used in succeeding years, with moderate success, was wardened by the RSPB during the nesting season.

The peregrine was harassed, mainly by those concerned with the preservation of gamebirds. Macpherson (1892) quoted a statement dated 1840 that two gamekeepers of the Earl of Lonsdale in Westmorland had "killed, young and old, not less than 18 of this species." Nelson (in his study of Yorkshire birds, 1907) reported: "Mr W Eagle Clarke visited an eyrie on the north-western fells [the Howgills] in 1880...The falcon was shot as she left her nest, which had 4 eggs, she being the sixteenth victim to the gun, all killed from eyries on this fell."

Bound for London

Thomas Pennant, in his *Tour of Scotland,* undertaken in the 1770s, heard how the London market was being supplied by large numbers of grouse and woodcock of Lakeland origin. He discovered that in the hills near Windermere were "numbers of springes for woodcocks, laid between tufts of heather, with avenues of small stones on each side to direct these foolish birds into the snares, for they will not hop over the pebbles. Multitudes are taken in this manner...and sent to the all-devouring capital by the Kendal stage."

Much remained. The author of *The History and Antiquities of Westmorland and Cumberland* (1777) noted that "about a mile south east from Sunbiggin in this manor is a lake called Sunbiggin Tarn, furnished (beside eels) with a brown trout not unlike char; where wild ducks also frequent and breed. The moors are generally furnished with grouse or Moor Game. And Orton Scar is famed for dotterels."

Kites and Harriers

To a Cumbrian, the red kite was known as "glad" or "glead." This elegant bird of prey with the rusty-red plumage, angled wings and deeply-forked tail, was for many years a familiar sight in the Lakeland sky. Clarke (1787) noted that it is "a native of this country and builds in trees." By his time, kites and other birds of prey were being culled. A pair of kites that nested in a tree near Ferry House, Windermere, was irresistible to one local worthy who shot the birds at the nest one moonlit night.

William Pearson (1780-1856), who lived at Borderside in the Winster valley, noticed that the kite appears "on windy days in autumn." Pearson considered that the "glead" had disappeared from the Lake District, though his old neighbour, Isaac Walker, remembered in his youth the pair that built yearly in "some lofty trees" near Ferry House. The kite also bred by Derwentwater and Ullswater.

Dorothy Wordsworth, sister of the Poet, visited Greenhead Gill in 1800 and saw "kites sailing above our heads." The last kite to be seen in Lakeland proper was shot at Portinscale in 1840. A kite that was slain near Carlisle in 1873 was sent to a taxidermist. Dixon Losh Thorpe bought the stuffed bird at a sale at Threlkeld of property belonging to the Sawyer family and in due course Ernest Blezard acquired the kite for the Tullie House collection at Carlisle. Ernest arranged for the "stuffing" to be renewed 90 years after the first operation that was performed by a local man using hay and something akin to red lead. The kite was partly mummified and, normally, would have disintegrated.

Harriers were scarce in Lakeland by 1830, though the buzzard remained "pretty common," even though many Lakeland farmhouses had stuffed birds on show and intrepid men like Isaac Colebeck, of Gosforth, went rock-climbing. He ascended Pillar Rock about the year 1847 and destroyed three nestlings. Pearson, writing about the year 1845, had not seen the species in the Winster valley for two or three years. About 12 nesting pairs were reported from Cumberland in 1885.

The crossbill, with its curious twisted beak and its partiality for conifer seeds, attracted the many collectors. When a pair was found nesting in the Alston area of the Pennines in 1839, the first reaction was to shoot the birds, which were presumably then preserved either as skins or "stuffed" specimens. A few pairs reputedly bred in the Lake District. In the winter of 1855-6, when the crossbill was unusually abundant in northern England, a Carlisle naturalist reported that "great numbers have been killed in various parts of Cumberland, Westmorland and Northumberland."

A Kendal ornithologist saw the crossbill occasionally, but records show that eggs were first taken in Lakeland in 1856 when James Fell, a slater, located a nest in a clump of fir-trees in the village of Cumwhinton, in the Eden Valley. Typically, the crossbills were nesting early in the year. Fell was intrigued by the birds when passing to and from his work. According to Macpherson. "after a short interval, he watched them building. At last, on the 20th of March, he climbed up to the nest and found that it contained four fresh eggs. He took the nest and its contents. T C Heysham purchased the nest and two eggs. The other two were disposed of to Thomas Armstrong, and have remained since in his cabinet." Crossbill eggs were removed from a nest in the fir woods on Penrith Beacon in 1865.

The Bird-Watchers

Eventually, birds were being observed as the result of scientific curiosity. During the Victorian period, when classification of birds and beasts was a principal concern, a bird in the hand was held to be more interesting than a bird in the bush. The first bird-watchers were interested in the life-style of their chosen species but were also, by and large, avid collectors of skins and eggs until quite recent times.

The bird most representative of the spirit of high and lonely places is the raven – a big bird, dressed in undertaker black, with croaky voice and an all-the-year-round presence. The Norse folk regarded it as sacred and Lakeland's poet, William Wordsworth, exhulted in its presence and, as far as the author knows, did not make a collection of eggs, though he did visit nests when he was a schoolboy at Hawkshead, recalling in his adulthood:

Oh! when I have hung
Above the raven's nest by knots of grass
And half-inch fissures in the slippery rock
But ill-sustained, and almost (so it seemed)
Suspended by the blast that blew amain,
Shouldering the naked crag…

Young Wordsworth saw bunches of unfledged ravens, on which rewards had been claimed, exhibited in the churchyard at Hawkshead. In 1782, at the age of 12, young Wordsworth and Tom Usher, "Taylor Tyson" Fletcher, William Rainscock of Rayrigg and others went to Yewdale Crags near Coniston to rob a raven's nest. Long before Wordsworth went bird-watching, a white raven, "bred in Cumberland," was put on display in London. The bird was seen by John Evelyn (1658). Sandford (1675) explained that Crosby

Ravensworth was so called "of the Ravens Timbring in the Timber Trees there, but now not a timber Tree standing."

What had been an awesome bird to the Norse settlers became quite simply a pest to the dalesfolk of later years. A headage payment for ravens was customary in Lakeland parishes. The Rev J Whiteside, in *Shappe in Bygone Days,* quotes that between 1718 and 1795 payment was 4d a bird. In 1784, Clarke (*Survey of the Lakes*) wrote: Ravens we have few, owing, I suppose, to the reward given for killing them. In Greystoke parish, between 1752 and 1842, headage payments were made on almost 1,000 ravens and, not surprisingly, by the end of that period the raven was reported to be "local" in Cumberland and nesting in "about a dozen localities."

A magpie was the subject of much superstition. Many Lakeland residents would count them in a traditional way:

One is for sorrow, but two for mirth,
Three's for a wedding, four for a death,
Five for heaven, six for hell,
But seven's the divil's oan sel'.

Early in the 18th century, Dr Robinson, "a learned divine," amused himself by observing the habits of rooks and other birds commonly seen in the haunts of man. He published his observations in two slim volumes entitled *Essay towards a Natural History of Westmorland and Cumberland* (1709). The 19th century was a great period for bird classification. J W Harris, a member of an old Quaker family of Cockermouth, collected (between 1860 and 1870) one or more specimens of every bird then on the British List. His collection became the nucleus of the one displayed at Tullie House, Carlisle, which was opened in 1893. In that year, a natural history society was formed in the city.

James Clarke, who was reared in the Ullswater district and became a land surveyor at Penrith, confessed to never becoming weary with his "researches into nature." He would set off, regardless of passing time, to explore the Lakeland fells, which were still the haunt of eagles. He wrote *A Survey of the Lakes of Cumberland, Westmorland and Lancashire* (1787) and in an appendix mentioned the presence in Lakeland of osprey as well as eagle. Lakeland parsons, well-educated men with a good deal of leisure time in which to indulge a favoured hobby, were prominent among the early Lakeland bird-watchers. The Rev W Richardson reported from first hand on the nesting of the golden eagle in Martindale in 1787 and 1789.

Medical practitioners were well-fitted by their training to take a scientific attitude towards a study of birds. Dr John Heysham, a young man who began to practise surgery in Carlisle in 1778, was soon devoting much of his leisure to ornithology. He believed the old adage that a bird in the hand was worth two in the bush and, having kept watch on a peregrine eyrie near Gilsland for five hours in 1781, he shot the returning female. Two years later, by the Lowther, he was studying pied flycatchers, trapping merlins at Rockcliffe by the Solway and keeping notes on hen harriers nesting at Newtown Common.

John Gough, born at Kendal in 1757, became blind but found ways of pursuing an interest in the natural world. Among his private papers was an essay on bird migration, dated 1812. His son, Dr Gough, made a considerable mark on the study of Lakeland fauna. In later life, despite a painful illness, he employed himself in writing a pamphlet entitled *Personal Reminiscences of the Habits of Animals*, sending a copy to Adam Sedgwick, a distinguished geologist who had been born and reared in Dentdale. Gough had twice introduced Sedgwick "into the scenes."

Carlisle, a city with a turbulent history and a rich natural setting, was home to some of the early naturalists, such as the aforementioned Dr John Heysham, a Lancastrian by birth, half Westmorland by parentage, and a Cumbrian by domicile. He was famed for his *Catalogue of Cumberland Animals*. His son, T C Heysham, who lived in Carlisle when taxidermy was the rage, was fascinated when he called on Mr Turner, the Penrith "bird-stuffer" on an October day in 1848 and saw the taxidermist was working on a nuthatch, which then was a scarce bird. This specimen had been taken on the banks of the Eamont and was reported to be common about Lowther.

The Rev H A Macpherson, who wrote a standard work, *The Vertebrate Fauna of Lakeland,* was fascinated – as were several notable Victorian naturalists - by the pied flycatcher, a summer visitor to our woodlands. Early observations on the species were made on the banks of the Kent near Levens Park (1793) and at Gowbarrow Park, beside Ullswater (1823) At a time when the impulses of migration were only dimly guessed at, Macpherson referred to the "constancy of purpose" with which "this little bird" annually crossed the Mediterranean, "hurries across the hot plain of Spain" and "threads its way through the mountain passes which debouch into Southern France." After crossing the Channel, the bird ultimately arrived in the "Lakeland glades" where "the sweet songs of many generations of pied flycatchers" had been heard.

Among the glamorous bird species of Lakeland – it being rare and found in remote places – was the dotterel, a plump little wading bird that winters by the Mediterranean and at nesting time is thinly spread across northern mountains. A trip [migratory flock] of dotterel occurred regularly in certain lowland areas, where it was greeted by a barrage of gunshot. These birds, being "fat and sweet-flavoured," were edible and anglers used dotterel feathers when tying "flies" to entice fish.

Captain Joseph Budworth, visiting Skiddaw towards the end of the 18th century, "saw some eight dotterel on the summit that let us approach within eighty yards; and, if I had not thrown a stone at them, I daresay I might have come near enough to have thrown salt on their tails..." Thomas Bewick noted that "the bird itself, when stripped of its plumage, sells for 4d., but its feathers at Keswick are always worth

6d." A dotterel egg from Skiddaw came into the possession of Dr John Heysham, of Carlisle, in 1785, and he penned the first-known description.

His son, Thomas Coulthard Heysham, having continued the family interest in dotterel, received a hamper from William Camm, of Keswick, in 1834. In the hamper were five dotterel, a note indicating that one bird had been alive when the hamper was packed. Camm apologised for the absence of dotterel eggs; though some shepherds were looking for them. John Cooper, who sought dotterel on behalf of Thomas Heysham, walked from Carlisle to Helvellyn, found the pair but not the nest, slept on the fell, located the nest early next morning and walked back to Carlisle with the eggs. William Hewitson found the nest of dotterel on Robinson. Nethersole-Thompson's monograph on the species (1973) estimates that, up to 1860, from 50 to 75 pairs nested in England, mainly in Cumbria. From 1927 onwards, dotterel nested sporadically.

In 1807, the farmers of the Penrith district revived the old idea of a headage payment for bird "pests." They clubbed together to pay a reward of tuppence per head for crow [in this case, rook] brought to them. They were anxious to safeguard their turnips and seed crops from the hungry birds.

The aforementioned Wordsworth is thought of as a poet, much given to musing. He was also an athletic person, devoted to landscape gardening and to fell-walking. In his travels through Lakeland, he had an ornithologist's eye and, as mentioned, was particularly fond of watching the raven. As he walked by Ullswater on a November day in 1805 he saw one such bird that was "not hovering like the kite, for that is not the habit of the bird; but passing onward with a straight-forward perseverance, and timing the motion of its wings to its own croaking. The waters were agitated; and the iron tone of the raven's voice, which strikes upon the ear at all times as the more dolorous from its regularity, was in fine keeping with the wild scene before our eyes.

At Grasmere, Rydal and most particularly on Elterwater – "the lake of the wild swans" – William and his sister had their spirits uplifted by wintering whoopers. In his day it was enough to refer to "wild swans." The mute swan was not often seen in Lakeland and the distinction between the whooper swan and its smaller, more northerly-nesting cousin, Bewick's swan, was not widely appreciated.

In 1892, William H Wintringham, an ornithologist with a profound love of the writings of William Wordsworth, delved in the Poet's work for references to birds. James Fisher in *The Shell Bird Book* (1966), who referred to this research, considered Wordsworth to be a true ornithologist, and a conservationist too. In 1810 he was advocating the designation of Lakeland as a sort of national property.

To Wordsworth, "the least motion which [birds] made...seemed a thrill of pleasure." To him, small birds warbled "to their paramours." Fisher remarked that he had not found "the aggressive secret uncovered earlier by White, but with earlier poets had *part* of the truth, there." Wordsworth's thrush was undaunted and constant in love. His blackbird was timid, the fieldfare pensive, the stonechat restless, the robin brisk and pious and tame – "the whole house is robin's cage."

The hedge sparrow was a little prattler, the blue tit a giddy sprite; the wren darkling and self-contented; the swallow fleet; the greenfinch like the dawning leaves; the linnet a singer in chorus; the jay affrighted; the magpie a chatterer; ravens were croakers, the crow lonely; the lark of the dawn, vigorous, buoyant, joyous but singularly carelessly ranged aloft; he put it in the sky, in clouds above, his head in sunbeams or a bowery cloud, in mid-air, on sun-gilt wing high poised, yet no higher than the pitch of "the inglorious football."

The swift was "by tender cares oppresst;" the nightjar solitary; the kingfisher flitting; the cuckoo blithe, a wandering voice, babbling, darling of the spring, a mystery, blessed. Wordsworth's barn owl was screeching, vagrant; the tawny owl shouting, hooting, silent; the golden eagle lord, flame-eyed; the white-tailed eagle lone and wailing.

Peregrines were found in clamorous agitation; the kite sailing; the buzzard shrill; the cormorant heavy, the heron silent, swans like sinless snakes, fair, mute, pure, bright, fitted to embrace, winding, glorying, unwearied. The snipe was darting and the sandpiper glancing. Gulls were white and sportive.

Bill Robson's researches into birds in the recent past deserve a mention; he was a farmer for six days a week and on the seventh day went out and about in field and on fell. He was born just before the 1914-18 war dramatically changed the social structure of rural areas, yet in his youth he still sampled the traditional Westmorland way of life and summer nights were still punctuated on the farms by the harsh double-call of the corncrake.

Bill and his naturalist friends formed the Eden Valley Field Club in 1954. He kept records of his bird observations and was entrusted by the British Trust for Ornithology to "ring" nestlings as part of the national study of bird migration. A tufted duck that Bill "ringed" at Sunbiggin Tarn in June, 1953, was shot at Wexford in Ireland eight months later. A mallard duckling handled in June, 1957, was picked up dead at Dinnington, Northumberland, in the following November. A swallow reared at Cote House, Warcop, died at Walvis Bay, on the West African coast, some 200 miles from the normal flight line, having been deflected off course by a sandstone.

To Bill Robson, the harbinger of spring was not the cuckoo but the ring ouzel, the upland version of the blackbird, returning in early April from its winter haunts on the Atlas Mountains of North Africa. Bill, listening to its cool, clear voice in the echo-chamber of a Lakeland gorge, regarded the bird as a northern nightingale. The dipper, which he studied intently from 1952 to 1964, was referred to by its Edenvale name of Bessy Dooker.

Bill claimed that the bird should be the avian emblem of Cumbria, favouring fast-flowing becks and also because the type specimen from which our British sub-species of dipper was identified was taken near

Penrith in 1801 and named by the naturalist *Latham Cinclus cinclus gularis.* As a person who studied the dipper, Bill thought of himself as being a cinclologist.

One of Bill's old schoolmates, Tommy Rudd, who worked at the Army range at Warcop, studied another aspect of birds – their calls and songs. Tommy built up such a fine collection of sounds that some of his recordings were accepted into the archives of the BBC. Among them was the double-syllable call, *whet-whet,* of the spotted crake, an uncommon, skulking species.

Bill Robson died as he had lived – out on the fells. His brother Jack had driven him to the foot of his chosen fell and arranged to pick him up at a prescribed time. He was overdue. A search team found Bill's body high up on his beloved Pennines, the haunt of raven, peregrine and buzzard. He lay not far from a patch of mountain everlasting, which was one of his favourite plants. The church at Warcop was packed for the funeral service. A sparrow joined the congregation and flew around the building as the parson recalled the life of a well-informed but modest naturalist.

Goldcrest

Meet the Birds

Crags and Ridges

The fell country of Lakeland bears a name derived from a Norse term, *fjell*. Today, it might be taken to mean any high, unimproved land, such as you will find if you walk the Fairfield horseshoe from Rydal and negotiate a succession of airy peaks. The high fell country has a sparse bird population but includes that grand trio of crag-nesting species – peregrine, raven and buzzard. (The last-named may still be found nesting on crags, often where a ledge has some protection from a rowan, but will be dealt with under woodland. The buzzard is now frequently found in tracts of old timber along the fell edges).

In your fell-country wanderings, you might also see a bird which looks impressive even from a distance, having a wing span of 6ft/2m. A pair of golden eagles has nested on crags overlooking Riggindale since the 1960s and, needing a large hunting area, may occasionally be seen in soaring flight by visitors using roads on either side, namely the cul de sac by Haweswater and Kirkstone Pass. Needless to say, the eyrie is wardened during the nesting season.

A walker sometimes becomes aware of the presence of a large bird of prey when he/she hears the honking of a carrion crow responding to the violation of its nesting territory. Incidentally, if you hear a loud outburst from a vegetated gully on high ground, do not look for something big. The songster will almost certainly be a common wren, one of the smallest birds on the British List.

The dotterel, one of the rarest of the British birds, nests spasmodically on mossy fell-tops both in Lakeland and on the northern Pennines. The swift, an urbanite, known to Lakers of old as "devilin," nests under the eaves at buildings in Lakeland towns and villages but might appear in its typical screaming flight over the highest ground, where it has a change of insect diet. Small and dark-brown, the bird cuts the air with wings shaped like scimitar blades. (In contrast, at Grange-over-Sands the ubiquitous swift might be seen gathering insect food as it hurtles along the shoreline or almost skims the tree-tops in nearby woods).

Raven

(Corvus corax)

Local name: Corbie

The raven is a big bird – the largest member of the crow family. It measures about 2ft from beak tip to tail and has a plumage of undertaker-black, though in bright light takes on some silvery highlights. The wings of this bird are long and narrow-ended. In flight they might appear to be slightly swept back. The throat of the raven is shaggy and the tail wedge-shaped. The normal flight call, a deep-throated "pruk, pruk," is distinguishable from the crow's call, being more of a hoarse croak.

Where the rocks of the Borrowdale Volcanics give Lakeland the dark grandeur of upjutting crags, you are more than likely to see a raven, maybe even a pair of ravens, playing hide-and-seek in the mist or riding the upthrust of air against rock without a single flap of their long wings. They are not restricted to the Volcanics but here the majority of the 80 or more pairs that nest in Lakeland are to be found, the crags having the deep ledges and cornices where they build their twiggy nests.

In addition to the established pairs, a floating population of ravens is made up of non-breeders. Such a floating population is thought to contain a surplus of potential breeders, for usually, if one of a nesting pair dies, its place is quickly taken by another.

Ravens will be found patrolling the ragged crest of Helm Crag near Grasmere and they follow the airy ridges of the Fairfield Horseshoe. Ravens glide and croak at Cautley Crag, the most dramatic feature of

Raven

the Howgill Fells above the upper Lune, and at High Cup Nick, on the northern Pennines, where nesting takes place on dolerite cliffs. Ravens sail the uprushing air currents just off the redstone cliffs of St Bees, on the Cumbrian coast. There is said to be a tree-nesting pair of ravens in wild country near Shap.

The raven, a most intelligent bird, seems to have a playful manner, flicking over on to its back and gliding upside down. It has a fine turn of speed when needed. At other times, it seems to dawdle in the air, a plaything of the wind. The aerobatics are most spectacular early in the year when ravens (having paired for life) renew their bonds. The male rises on a thermal, then tucks in his wings and makes a steep descent. The pair circle each other or fly so close their wing-tips are almost brushing. Then, being ravens, they will show off by flicking on their backs and flying upside down for a short distance.

A well-established pair of ravens does not vacate its nesting crags the year through, except when the young of the year are being coaxed towards independence. During much of the summer, a family travels as a party and reaches places far distant from the nest. The young ravens gain in confidence, mastery of the air and self-reliance. After about three months, the young disperse and the nesting pair return to their territory.

Over 30 crags in Lakeland are named after the raven. Early in the year – and sometimes when the fells are white over with snow – a raven pair makes a selection from several previously used nesting sites on its territory. The birds engage in their exciting air displays, flipping on their backs or diving with closed wings. In recent years, their territorial rights have been violated by peregrines, a species that was formerly scarce and tended to winter at the coast. Now the peregrines are more numerous, and inclined in mild winters to stay in the breeding areas, the ravens have unacceptable competition.

Within a raven territory there may be one or two sites that are used in rotation. A raven nest is bulky composed largely of coarse twigs, including hawthorn, rowan and heather, lined with softer material, including sheep wool. A bird might be sitting eggs before the end of February. Whatever the weather, the brooding bird is able to maintain a high temperature in the deep pocket of the nest.

The eggs, usually five in number, are bluish-green with brown spots but a raven pair that nested near Windermere was celebrated because the female produced red eggs, which were much sought after by collectors. The eggs are incubated for about three weeks and the fledglings are nestbound for around six weeks, being fed on gobbets of carrion. Their period of greatest hunger occurs when there is plenty of carrion in the upper dale country. Lambing time is in full swung. The ravens benefit from those sheep and lambs that have succumbed to adverse conditions.

A raven is not unusually shy and when a walker enters its territory it will glide swiftly along the edge of the cliffs or, during the nesting season, alight and peevishly tug up pieces of grass, tossing them into the breeze.

Ravens attend communal roosts in winter. Ernest Blezard counted 60 birds at one roost. He also examined castings [the indigestible parts of meals that are ejected in the form of pellets] and found sheep wool and bones. A Borrowdale raven had ingested 16 pieces of quartz to help with the digestion.

A fine monograph on the raven has been written by Derek Ratcliffe, a native of Carlisle who became a chief scientist of the Nature Conservancy. He noted that the raven, a common and even cherished scavenger of our medieval towns, had become by the end of the 19th century "an outcast creature of the lonely places, the sheep walks, moorlands, mountains and rugged seaboard." The raven's large, powerful bill has sharp-edged mandibles, the upper being curved and almost hooked at the tip, enabling it to both strike heavy blows and tear at flesh.

Anyone who falls under the spell of the raven through watching it in wild haunts invests it with romance. Ratcliffe mentions the Norse regard for it. To them it was a sacred bird. A legend concerning the war-god Odin mentioned that he had two ravens, named Hugin and Munin (Thought and Memory). Each day they flew all over the world to gather information. In the evening, they sat on Odin's shoulders and related to him what they had heard and seen.

Golden Eagle

(Aquila chrysaetos)

Rare

If you are in two minds about whether the large soaring bird is an eagle or a buzzard – then it's a buzzard. The golden eagle, which is appreciably larger, is named from the pale gold feathers of the head, but this is unlikely to be seen in normal conditions, especially when the bird is airborne. Then the appearance of a mature bird is one of general brownness. (An immature bird shows white on the wings and the tail-base). As a golden eagle rises in a thermal, its broad wings are held in a shallow arch. Eventually, the huge bird may be little more than a small dark form against cloud. An eagle likes plenty of space. A friend of the author picked up a moulted eagle feather under an isolated thorn where the big bird had apparently been resting.

An observation hide in Riggindale, approached along a path from the head of Haweswater, is within viewing range of an eyrie, which is situated on a rock ledge. A log-book contains details of eagle activity. The author was fortunate when, from this vantage point, he espied two eagles and a pair of agitated peregrines in the same limited air space.

Seeing an eagle is a matter of chance. Eagles breakfast early and then, if hunting has been good, might rest up for many hours. Live food up to the size of red grouse or hare is taken, with the hunting eagle quartering the ground at no great height, ready to drop on any luckless creature that breaks cover. Or the bird might gorge itself on carrion, such as a dead sheep. Having had a good meal, the bird will perch for a long period before the next phase of activity.

A hunting eagle has been seen by visitors who kept watch from the cul-de-sac road beside Haweswater. Even more impressive is the nuptial display of eagles, which alternately swoop and glide with aplomb. Nesting begins early in the year and the eggs, usually two in number, are being incubated by March. There is a protracted fledgling period. The eaglet that emerges from the first egg to hatch can show such savagery to its nest-mate that the other dies. One lusty infant is reared. Unfortunately, in Lakeland, the old pair seem to be getting too old for successful breeding.

Dotterel

(Charadrius morinellus)

Rare

When dotterel fly north from their wintering grounds near the Mediterranean, these plump little waders exchange their drab brown plumage for nuptial attire. Now the crown is dark and a white band is prominent over each eye, meeting in a V at the back of the head. A grey breast is separated by a bold white band from the red-chestnut of the belly. A lively trill is heard from dotterel on take-off. On the hilltops where the dotterel nests, what might seem like a conspicuous plumage has a cryptic coloration. The plumage of the female is much brighter than that of the male because after mating she leaves the nesting routine and the rearing of the young to her partner.

The first dotterel to arrive are in small groups, known as "trips," which are in passage, most of them to far northern nesting grounds. Dotterel have been seen on spring migration on our estuaries and also at Sunbiggin Tarn, in the limestone country near Orton, this remote tract of water being a favourite with many migratory species. Pendle, a "flat top" overlooking the Ribble Valley (and, in clear weather, the

Lake District) is a place where dotterel rest and feed. The first birds arrive in mid-April, but the best viewing time is early-May, the birds resuming their journey at the middle of the month. Over 30 dotterel were seen on Pendle in 1988.

Breeding in the Lake District and on the Northern Pennines is spasmodic and to interfere is a serious breach of the bird protection law. The dotterel has been known as "fool of the moss" from its confiding manner but by sitting tight the bird ensures that its eggs will not be frosted in the extreme climatic conditions of high ground.

Peregrine

Falco peregrinus

Local name: Blue Hawk

The male peregrine, with its mantle of RAF blue and moustachial stripe, has the dashing manner of Flying Officer Kite, an archetypal RAF officer. As the peregrine lies on the wind, notice a cigar-shaped body and swept-back wings. In good light, barring is evident on the light underparts. The tail of this bird is relatively short. When their nesting territory has been violated,

peregrines give a chattering kek-kek-kek-kek.

The Lake District is a stronghold of the peregrine and pairs are well distributed. Nesting takes place in quarries as well as on natural cliffs. The peregrine, largest of the falcons, with long wings that give the bird both speed and power, was much prized by the falconers of old. They called the female "falcon" and the male "tiercel," which means one third smaller. There *is* a difference in size, but not to such an extent.

Plump and muscular, the peregrine has been described as the ultimate flying machine. It is also a true crag-nester, using a broad ledge and depositing its red eggs in a depression with scarcely any nesting material. The stoop [dive] of a peregrine on its prey, usually a medium-sized bird like a pigeon, has been estimated to exceed 100 mph. (Some years ago, a peregrine on the Eastern Fells of Lakeland was seen stooping at a bright green bird that turned out to be a stray parrot from a wildlife park).

For centuries, fledgling falcons were taken for falconry. The Middleton family held their land in the upper Lune by annual rendering of a cast of falcons to my lord at Kendal Castle. Following breeding failures in the 1940s, the peregrine population declined in the 1950s, along with other bird-eating raptors, when they ingested a residue of highly toxic insecticides used in agriculture. The peregrine, at the head of the food chain, suffered badly. A voluntary ban on the use of such chemicals as aldrin and dieldrin as seed-dressings was introduced in 1962.

The peregrine population recovered to the extent that now virtually all the traditional sites are occupied and, as mentioned, some pairs are taking over traditional raven sites. Usually, peregrines that wintered at the coast returned to their nesting sites in March. The young are able to leave the nest in early July.

Meadow Pipit

(Anthus pratensis)

The meadow pipit, one of the "little brown jobs" encountered during a jaunt on the hills, is worthy of a second glance. It is a dainty little bird, not unlike a small version of the song thrush, having a brown mantle and whitish underparts, streaked on the upper breast and flanks.

The meadow pipit is a restless bird with a jerky flight. The cock bird often draws attention to itself by its song flight, during which it soars, then descends, still warbling, with stiffened wings and tail. This has been described as a "shuttlecock" flight. The nest is often revealed when a sitting bird leaves at the very last moment, almost at a walker's feet.

The humble meadow pipit, the commonest bird on the fells in summer, is the favourite food of the merlin and is frequently selected as a foster parent by the cuckoo. It maintains its numbers by dint of having a long nesting season during which two, sometimes three, broods are reared.

The **tree pipit** occurs where a fellside is thinly spread with trees. To anyone with scant knowledge of birdlife, it is another of the "little brown jobs." The only way a walker might distinguish it from a meadow pipit is in its proneness to undertake a song flight from (and back to) a branch or post.

Skylark

(Alauda arvensis)

This ordinary-looking bird is one of our chief songsters. From high in the sky, the cock bird pours out an unending torrent of rapturous notes. The skylark is appreciably larger than a pipit. Notice its head-crest (which is often raised).

On some of the grassy Lakeland fells, such as between Haweswater and Ullswater, skylarks are still quite common. On a summer day, a walker passes from one lark territory to another with a sweet warbling accompaniment all the way.

The female constructs a nest within a hollow depression and she alone incubates the eggs. The male bird joins in the feeding of the young which, leaving the nest in about 10 days, become airborne about 10 days later. The breeding season is long enough to permit the raising of two or three broods.

Wren, Common

(Troglodytes troglodytes)

Local name: Chitty

Generally distributed on low ground, this restless, noisy little bird, scarcely four inches long, may also be found in wild settings such as the crags above Honister Pass or around the head of Wasdale. The appearance is familiar to older people, if only from the image on the old-time farthing. Notice the bird's large head, brown coloration and the cocked-up tail.

Anyone who is unfamiliar with the vehement song of the wren will stare with disbelief on locating the tiny songster. The eyesight must be keen to follow the movements of this diminutive bird among the rocks.

The scientific name implies "cave dweller," which is hardly the case, though the tucked-away nest is domed. The cock bird laboriously builds up to a dozen nests, using dry grass, leaves and moss, but leaving them unlined. The female then makes a final choice and provides a feather lining.

Snow Bunting

(Plectrophenax nivalis)

A scattering of little birds that are predominantly white, with especially long wings, are almost certainly snow buntings, immigrants from the far north. The snow bunting has so much white on its plumage that in its buoyant flight across a wintry landscape it resembles a snowflake, especially as a flock is content with a ragged formation, with each bird flying, settling or hopping over the snow as it pleases. The birds dine on seeds of grasses which in snowtime protrude from the snow.

The nearest nests of snow buntings are on the Cairngorms in Scotland and even there the species nests fitfully. Most of our winter visitors are from Iceland. Birds in passages forage at various points on the coast, including Ravenglass, where three little rivers blend their waters in a muddy area, and at South Walney and Foulney, two of the islands of Morecambe Bay that are now connected to the mainland by bridge or causeway.

To see a flock of snow buntings on a high and otherwise lifeless fell that is streaked by snow and swept by a cutting wind is a sight of joyful remembrance.

Ring Ouzel

(Turdus torquatus)

Local name: Crag starling

This visitor for nesting is also known as "mountain blackbird," having a superficial resemblance to the familiar garden bird but being found at an elevation of over 1,000ft. The male sports a conspicuous white gorget [crescent] on its breast and the breast takes a silvery sheen from white outer lines to the breast feathers. This gives them a scaly effect. The female, who has the main nesting duties, is comparatively dull, being brownish. The gorget is less well defined. First year females have a mottled breast.

A fell-walker might hear the somewhat repetitive song as he/she boots-up at the car park near the head of Haweswater. Local fells, being rocky, carry several pairs of ring ouzels. At close quarters, the bird is clever at losing itself among rocks and patches of bracken.

Our ring ouzels, after wintering in North Africa and southern Spain, return to Lakeland in late March and early April, the males arriving one or two weeks before the females and all moving directly to their nesting areas. Singing by the male ouzels is loud, fluty and repetitive. It becomes intense as rivalry between males is evident. Wing-fluttering is part of the display when one bird attempts to ward off the attentions of a rival. The alarm call is a harsh *chook, chook, chook.*

The nest, constructed from dead bracken and rough grasses, with a lining of finer grasses, is set on a rocky ledge low down in a gill, quarry, wall or derelict building. Double-breeding takes place in a favourable season. The ring ouzel is more common on the Northern Pennines, where birds favour narrow rocky gills, also valleys with steep sides in which streams occur. Nests have been found at around 1,500 ft/460m.

Before the ring ouzel leaves for its wintering quarters, in early autumn, parties of birds up to 60 strong move along the fellsides and feed on the berries of rowan, thorn and juniper. When birds have been dining on bilberries, their droppings take on a deep purple hue.

Wheatear

(Oenanthe oenanthe)

Local name: White-rump

This fidgety little bird, a summer visitor, has a smart stance when it is

momentarily still as it perches on boulder or drystone wall. The male, which is most conspicuous, is blueish-grey on its crown and mantle, with a black patch on the eye and light underparts. The name wheatear has nothing to do with the cereal but relates to the bird's white rump, as the old Lakeland name implies. The male has a brief warbling song. The alarm call is a harsh "tak," like the sound made by two stones being struck together.

The male wheatears arrive towards the end of March, the females turning up a week or two later. This species is hyperactive and when not engaged in looking for insect food seems to use up surplus nervous energy with a bobbing action and much flicking of wings and tail.

The wheatear is with us a long time, dispersing to winter quarters in late August and September. This is a bird of "broken" ground that nests at even greater elevations than the ring ouzel. You may find it among a jumble of rocks and coarse vegetation in a high-lying corrie. Also look for it where there is rocky ground at lower elevations.

Moor and Dalehead

Lakeland has comparatively little heather moor, of the quality one might find on the northern Pennines, but there are tracts of heather and other areas where overgrazing by sheep has, as on the Pennines, left a dreadful legacy of Nardus grass. A big empty area lies "back o' Skidder [Skiddaw]." Roads cross some extensive moorland between the Duddon Valley and the coastal strip.

The heads of some major Lakeland dales are not as constricted as you might think, for here there are alluvial plains, of material washed down from the fells and left in such a level state they might have been created using a spirit-level. A good example of such a dalehead is Great Langdale.

Merlin

(Falco columbarius)

This thrush-sized raptor nests on the ground beneath moorland heather. The male has a grey back; the female is larger than her mate and has a mantle of brown. A merlin dines on pipits and larks, captured during a swift, low flight sustained by short but pointed wings and short tail. In winter, merlins resort to the low country, notably the coastal marshes, where there are concentrations of small birds on which to prey.

Merlins are back on the moors in April and in the following month have clutches of eggs, both birds sharing the incubation duties. The eggs hatch quite late in the year, when there is a glut of young larks and pipits. The male brings such food to the female to be fed to the young.

Black Grouse

(Tetrao tetrix)

The male, known as the blackcock, is large, podgy, dark, with conspicuous red wattles. The smaller female (greyhen) is not unlike the red grouse in appearance, though lacks the white feathering on the legs.

Blackcock have their traditional leks [assembly areas] where each bird has its territory and, in spring, display in pairs, testing each other's mettle by their posturing, by flaring their wattles, drooping their wings and spreading their white under-tail coverts. The calls at a lek include dove-like cooing and explosive hisses. Such a lek is (in many cases was) visited at other times and, up to the end of April, has a less intense afternoon performance.

The most successful birds at the lek gain the central positions where they are most likely to catch the eye of visiting greyhens. The females, when mated, are ignored and, without help, attend to nesting, incubating the eggs and attending to the chicks.

The black grouse, now scarce, favour areas, between moorland and forest, where there is a mix of trees, some open ground and areas of bogland. The species used to be relatively common in Grizedale, Kentmere, Haweswater and also on the Solway Mosses. A larger population occurred on the northern Pennines. Efforts are being made in selected areas to provide the conditions in which black grouse might thrive so that the species might recover its former prominence.

Red Grouse

(Lagopus lagopus)

Local name: Moorcock

The appearance of the red grouse is well-known, if only from pictures on whisky bottles. The species has a rotund shape with a small head. The cock

bird has red eye wattles that are inflated during courtship and territorial disputes. The plumage is a shiny, rufous-brown, with a white wing round the eye and a moustachial stripe. A wide range of calls includes, most commonly, "kowa, kowa," which has a curious human quality and sounds like "go back, go back." The hen grouse, smaller and lighter coloured than the cock, is yellowish with dark barring in the breeding season, being thus well camouflaged in the moorland setting.

The red grouse is virtually a prisoner in a calluna landscape, its digestive system having been evolved to deal with a diet of tough, fibrous heather shoots. The bird takes into its gizzard a quantity of quartz grit with which it can grind the heather. Moorland seeds and fruits are taken in season.

The species is relatively common where heather moors are well-maintained. It occurs in Skiddaw Forest, also heathery tracts above Borrowdale and on Shap, but the finest grouse moors are those lying at about 1,250 ft on the Pennines. Here the rank heather is periodically burnt (swizzened) to encourage the growth of fresh shoots for grouse and sheep. Grouse chicks are precocious and by late July they weigh almost as much as the adults.

Golden Plover

(Pluvialis apricaria)

Local name: Pennine Whistler

When the golden plover returns to the fells to nest, it is resplendent in its nuptial plumage, which consists of golden speckling above and (below a conspicuous white band) dark underparts. Birds of the southern race, which nest in northern England, are not as boldly marked on the underparts as the northern race birds, which are jet black. The golden plover moves with mincing steps, utters a mournful whistle – "too-ee" – and is quick to detect intrusion, moving away from the nest and by its movements confusing the intruder.

Lakeland has comparatively few pairs of this upland wader; they nest mainly in the north and east. The golden plover likes a relatively bare landscape. The wastes back o'Skiddaw and the Caldbeck and Shap fells hold a few pairs. The moors above the dales of Esk and Duddon hear the melancholic call. The best places to see the golden plover are on the northern Pennines, especially where there is broken ground. They have been known to nest on Cross Fell, the highest hill on the range.

South Walney is one of the wintering grounds for golden plover of the northern race. When the birds colour up before their northward migration for nesting, the jet-blackness of the underparts is conspicuous.

Carrion Crow

(Corvus corone)

Local name: Dope or Doup

Despite its sinister reputation, the carrion crow is a handsome as well as an intelligent bird. The plumage is black. So is the beak and the coarse hairs that show prominently at the base. The feathers do not carry the high gloss of the rook, with which it might be confused, both being prone to feed in open fields. The voice is a somewhat angry cawing, compared with the more languid caw of the rook and the metallic jabbering of jackdaws.

Every dalesman's hand has been against the carrion crow, mainly because of the way it attacks injured or ailing lambs in spring. It is also accused of taking game birds. A self-respecting gamekeeper had no crows on his territory because he shot those that came within range and dislodged any crow nests from trees with the help of a long rod known as a "crow poker." In some cases, a gamekeeper used a captive bird in a cage to entice other crows into captivity – and death.

Today, the persecution of the crow has virtually ended. With far fewer gamekeepers, the population has been left to find its own level. The carrion crow has become cheeky, if not confiding. You might walk within a short distance of perched or feeding birds without causing them to take wing.

Crows nest in isolated trees, such as the old thorn tree on an otherwise bare hillside. The bird has been known to nest on wall-tops. A twiggy structure may have sheep bones worked into it and the eggs or young recline on a lining of sheep's wool. Should the nestlings, which are naked and helpless, detect a movement near the nest, they raise their rubbery necks and open their beaks to reveal a reddish gape, all the time giving strident hunger-calls.

A pair of crows keeps strictly to itself when nesting but at other times the crow seems happy when socialising, especially at prime food sources and a winter roost.

Jackdaw

(Corvus monedula)

This jaunty bird is the smallest of the crow family. The plumage is black above and grey on the nape, shoulders and underparts. The sharp, metallic call – "jack" – becomes a noisy chorus if the birds are disturbed at their nesting area or are flying out of their winter roost to forage in fields and villages. They also ransack urban litter-bins.

Jackdaws nest communally, if possible, such as in cracks in the face of an old quarry or even a redundant field barn. Nesting in church towers is to be noted where churchwardens have not sealed points of entry with wire mesh. Special wire cowls are used to deter jackdaws from nesting in the chimneys of houses which now have other forms of heating than coal fires. They collect so many large twigs for the nest that when removed by the owner of the property they sometimes fill a sack.

Kestrel

(Falco tinnunculus)

Local name: Windhover

The kestrel, our commonest bird of prey, has achieved celebrity as the bird that hovers when looking for food. You are just as likely to see the "wind-hover" at the roadside or even in an urban area as in remote country. A close view of the hovering bird reveals long pointed wings and a long tail with a black terminal band. Both male and female are coloured reddish-brown above, with lighter (and heavily spotted) underparts. The head and tail are tinted grey. Both birds have a natty black "moustache." The kestrel occasionally utters a rasping call.

The female kestrel is slightly larger than the male but you are not likely to be able to use this piece of information in field conditions where a tape measure is not available.

In normal flight, the bird has short spells of wing-flapping and gliding. Then it has the general appearance of a sparrowhawk, which is of a similar size. After hovering, and detecting a luckless mammal (or bird), the kestrel swoops steeply for the kill.

Barn Owl

(Tyto alba)

Now an uncommon bird, the barn owl looks pale, almost ghostly, as it hunts for small mammals in the gloaming. The wings beat slowly (and silently), the eyes being like black grapes in a large heart-shaped face and the owl's ears tuned to the rustling in the ground vegetation that signifies food. Notice, when the owl flies, there are frequent changes of pace and direction. The legs tend to dangle. Now and again, a barn owl gives a blood-curdling screech.

The species is well-named, for it nests mainly in outbuildings. The ghostly plumage consists of sandy-brown, flecked with darker marks, forming a delicate pattern, above. The underparts are of pure white feathers. On no account disturb barn owls by entering their nesting quarters. If this is in a barn, watch from a distance as an adult bird flies out for food and returns with a small mammal, usually a vole, grasped in one of its talons.

The owlets give a rhythmic hissing sound – almost like snoring – to stimulate their parents to go hunting for food. Young birds go through two changes of plumage and then emerge into the open with immaculate attire. The parents, having run a shuttle-service with food several times during the night, become somewhat careworn and overwhelmed when, arriving back at the nesting quarters, they are mobbed by eager youngsters. Like other members of the owl family, the barn owl eats its small mammal prey whole and then regurgitates the indigestible parts in the form of pellets which, to a naturalist, are an excellent source of

Barn Owl

information on what the bird eats.

Some barn owls, when flying low as they seek food, are injured by road traffic. A shortage of nesting places has been partly overcome by providing boxes in otherwise suitable buildings.

Swallow

(Hirundo rustica)

A familiar summer visitor, the swallow usually nests in farm buildings and even on beams in church porches, where boards are attached to collect the droppings. Notice, when you have a close view of the swallow, that it has a glossy blue back, a chestnutty hue on the forehead and throat and white underparts. In flight, the swept-back wings and long tail streamers are conspicuous.

The appearance of the swallow in April is a cause of rejoicing. The male bird is the first to arrive, invariably finding a nesting site used previously. If last year's mate has survived the stresses of migration, she will join him. Otherwise he finds another mate.

In May, the birds are nesting, the nest being built on a ledge, such as a beam. A feather lining is provided. Two broods are usual and sometimes a third brood is attempted.

For such an attractive bird, the swallow utters what one observer referred to as "grating twitters." It sings loud and long when airborne or at rest. Swallows congregate on telephone wires as the days chill and they prepare to return to their wintering quarters in South Africa.

The closely-related **house martin** is blue-black above, white beneath. This species is smaller, with shorter wings, than the swallow. The tail is forked but lacks streamers. The main distinguishing feature is a white rump. As its name implies, it is seen in built-up areas where it collects pellets of mud and pieces of straw for a nest which it attaches to suitable places under the eaves or in the corners of windows.

Curlew

(Numenius arquata)

Local name: Whaup

The largest of the European waders has a streaky-brown plumage, long legs and a long, downcurved bill that is useful for deep probing in mud and may also be used delicately for picking up tit-bits of food from ground level. The bill of a female curlew is appreciably longer than that of the male. The (very familiar) contact call is a rousing "cour-loo," with the accent on the first syllable. The song, which is heard as the bird flies round its territory in spring, begins with slow measured notes that rise in pitch and tempo to become a sequence of bubbling phrases.

The curlew, a visitor for nesting, is the true harbinger of spring in the northern fell-country. As a farmer remarked: "I reckon t'back o' winter is broken when I hear a curlew shout." It is a ground-nester that once was common in the meadows of the dale. Changes in the form of drainage, re-seeding and the use of artificial fertilisers have changed the preferred habitat of such birds as curlew and lapwing, robbing them of food and cover.

A wary bird, the curlew is aggressive when its nest is threatened, as by crows, on which it dives with a loud call and whoosh of displaced air. The curlew is not common today but is best seen towards the east of the Lake District and along the East Fellside of the Eden Valley.

Curlews and other wading birds might be commonly seen along muddy stretches of the Cumbrian coast in winter. If you hear a curlew-ish snatch of sound inland in winter – look out for that prime mimic, the starling.

Lapwing

(Vanellus vanellus)

Local names: Peewit, Teufit

In its nuptial plumage, the dark back and wings have a greenish gloss – hence green plover, another name for the species. The face and throat are patterned black and white. Notice a prominent head crest. There is a dark breast band. The belly is white and the under-tail coverts a rich chestnut. The most familiar call is a rather plaintive "pee-wi."

The lapwing is an early visitor for nesting and winters by the coast. This is the bird that has an exuberant display flight, tumbling to the ground in wild abandon – and pulling out of the dive when it seems as though it is about to crash. The plaintive call is evocative of wild and lonely fellsides.

The north of England now has the largest population of lapwings, a species that has declined greatly inland but is still a moderately common nester on coastal marshes. The lapwing has nested at up to about 1,200 ft on Lakeland hills, using ground with gentle gradients, but will be more familiar to bird-watchers visiting Edenvale and the Pennines.

When there was a goodly number of nesting lapwings, they tended to nest in loose colonies where the moist ground – known to many a dalesman as "tewit-grund" – provided food and cover.

Fieldfare

(Turdus pilaris)

A visitor from Scandinavia in winter, the fieldfare is a large thrush with a pale plumage. When a flock is disturbed, it flies off in a low straggly formation. Notice the powder-blue head and rump, chestnut back and wings and spotted breast. In its winter plumage, it looks paler than this description implies. The frosty flight call – "chak-chak" – is appropriate to the bird's northern haunts.

Fieldfares are colonial nesters in their frosty northern lands. When they have consumed the rowan berries in their natal areas, they cross the North Sea, usually having an East Coast landfall by night. At first they dine on worms and insects. They then harvest the berries – mainly haws, from the hawthorn, but also rowan, holly, even ivy.

Fieldfares thus lead a nomadic life at the dictates of the food supply, which they must share with their cousins, the redwings – which are also refugees from the hard far-northern winter – and with blackbirds and mistle thrushes.

The **redwing**, smallest of the thrush family you will see in the Lake District, is named after a red-brown patch which is actually under the wing. Part of it is visible on the flanks. It is slimmer than the fieldfare and has a noticeable white eye-stripe. You may be fortunate to hear the calls of redwings – a thin "see, see" – in nocturnal flight. At the winter roost, they noisily sing themselves to sleep.

Goldfinch

(Carduelis carduelis)

This pretty little bird with a red white and black head and flashing gold-barred wings is much more common than it was, having hitherto been prized as a cage bird.

Goldfinches nest quite late and feed their young on mashed-up thistle seeds which are not available until about the beginning of June. They can produce as many as three broods and by the end of August the countryside appears full of families dining on thistles and roadside and garden plants that are seeding. They might be seen plucking at the seeds of dandelion clocks.

A southward migration takes many goldfinches to Spain. Others remain in the home areas. Towards the end of winter charms [flocks] of goldfinches may have a strength of 30 and more. In winter they are partial to black sunflower seed feeders. They have even been known to take peanuts.

Woodland, Forest and Scrub

The highest-situated individual trees are rowan, thorn and holly. Of native woodland, oak and birch are locally common. Although sessile oakwood became the climax vegetation in the Lake District, there has been severe moderation through the activities of man and also his sheep, which by their intense grazing left such woodland deficient in shrub layer.

Oakwoods, with trees of various ages, extending in elevation to over 1,000 ft, are the nesting haunts of buzzard, chaffinch, willow warbler and blackbird. Eric Simms, a naturalist who grew up at Appleby, and wrote and broadcast widely about bird life, once referred to the "scrubby woods" on Lakeland hillsides where willow warblers and chaffinches sing, and also the "steamy damp oakwoods" where he found redstarts and wood warblers "bringing to the hillsides some of the loveliest sounds of northern England." The pied flycatcher, and coal tits, are among the most typical birds of the fell woods. Bird life is most varied and numerous where there are mixed species of trees with some good cover.

Lakeland has some notable beech woodland, such as in the Grasmere-Rydal area, where you might find a wintering flock of bramblings, these being finches, not unlike chaffinches. They consort with each other. The cock brambling has a pale rump and less white on its wings and tail. The shy hawfinch occurs on the outskirts of woods (listen for a *tick* note, uttered in flight). Irritatingly, the hawfinch, a dumpy bird with an enormous bill, brown back, grey neck and pink-brown underparts, spends much of its time in the tree tops, so it hardly flaunts its fine plumage before the gaze of human watchers. At least one Lakeland housewife living near woodland has been astonished to see this species appear at the bird table. The woodland of the Rusland Valley, Monk Coniston and Grizedale Forest, also oak woods on the western side of Windermere, are places where you might be alert for the *tick, tick* of this distinctive bird.

Winter bird-watching in woodland is less frustrating than in summer. With the leaves fallen, you can at least see what is present. In the birch/alder woodland, as by Rydal Water, look out for mixed flocks of birds, including redpoll, known in West Cumberland as Banty Hemplin, and siskin. The last-named is lively and small, the cock bird being a bright yellowish-green. Though the hedge sparrow (known to Lakers of old as Creepydyke) has a name associating it with farmland, and is a familiar bird of large gardens, this species and the robin are birds characteristic of the old north-country wildwood.

Another bird seen in winter is the long-tailed tit. This species nests in Lakeland and a pair builds, in bramble or hawthorn, one of the most elaborate nests in the bird world. Their structure, set on a platform of moss, involves three layers – lichen (outside), grass and moss (the next layer) and around 2,000 feathers (for the lining). The nest is delicately bound together using such materials as the cocoons of spiders. The structure expands with the growth of the family within.

Man's blanket planting of alien trees changed the appearance of Lakeland. Larch was a favourite in the 18th and 19th centuries. Wordsworth, writing at the time of the Industrial Revolution, dismissed what were then the new plantations as "vegetable manufactury." An early afforestation scheme with conifers was undertaken around Thirlmere by Manchester Corporation before the 1914-18 war. The Forestry Commission blanketed many a fellside with alien conifers, mainly sitka spruce, from north-west America. When European larch was planted, its foliage, cast in winter, brought blessed relief to the monotonous appearance of massed spruce.

Although it was agreed there should be no planting in central Lakeland, this was not always observed and it is only in recent times that the stark appearance has been moderated by using a variety of species, both coniferous and deciduous trees. At Grizedale Forest, the Commission's showplace, there is a goodly variety of tree species – and a varied fauna. Incidentally, do not despise the woodpigeon (known in Lakeland as cushat), which is common in wooded situations. If a bird takes (noisy) flight, its leathery wings beating vigorously, you may find yourself looking up at its frail nest, in which the number of twigs seems meagre and occasionally you can actually see the eggs from below!

Buzzard

(Buteo buteo)

Local name: Shreak

Big, overall brown, thick neck, broad but blunt wings and widely-spread tail – these are identification points for the buzzard. The bird has a loud and cheery flight call – peeioo, peeioo. It sounds rather like the mewing of a cat. When a buzzard is viewed from beneath, which is usually the case, notice that the general brown is offset by white patches towards the outer end of each wing.

The bird which often shouts to be noticed may be seen circling on its broad but blunt wings over a ridge or floating over the green mantle of a hillside deciduous wood. Use a roadside parking spot between

Windermere and Kirkstone for a view of the upper Troutbeck Valley and, perhaps, a downward view of a buzzard above the straggly oak-woods.

The buzzard has a reputation for laziness but is actually a skilled hunter and does not often deign to pick up dead meat. The buzzard circling above a Lakeland valley may appear languid but its eyes are taking up even quite small prey items at a range of up to two miles. This bird's eyesight is astonishing, the eyes being equivalent in size to those of a human being. The bird trims its wings and tail to the air currents, minimising the effort involved in flight.

The much-persecuted buzzard made its last stand by nesting on rock ledges, often those screened by a rowan tree growing from a crack in the rock. A relaxation in keepering, and a more enlightened opinion about the role of raptors in the natural scheme, has been followed by tree-nesting in woodland. The food-hunting area is mainly rough ground between the open fells and woodland.

In early spring, courting buzzards put on a stunning display of flight. They make circles just above the female, keeping her face in full view and periodically diving and swooping at close quarters – so close that their talons momentarily join. At such a time the mewing sound is constant. The buzzard seldom lays eggs before the end of April, and even then it may have to withstand falls of snow.

The bird dines on young birds and small mammals but also visits dead sheep. When, in the 1970s, myxomatosis claimed most of the rabbits in the Duddon Valley, buzzards resorted to mice, voles, beetles, grass snakes, adders and even fish stranded by the river. At the time of writing, the Lakeland rabbit population is high – and so is the number of buzzards. Birds are colonising areas to the east of their old range.

Jay

(Garrulus glandarius)

This large member of the crow family is more often heard than seen. The chattering call is reflected in its scientific name – garrulus. The jay has black and white feathers on the crown, which is erectile, forming a distinctive crest. The bird's body is coloured pinkish-brown, though is darker on the back. Look out for a white rump with a contrasting black tail.

Walk in any of the mixed deciduous woods of Central Lakeland, or in a parkland area like that between Ambleside and Rydal Hall, and you may hear the screech of a jay.

In autumn, this large and colourful bird is at its most conspicuous, hopping on the ground, seeking acorns. At close quarters, the white and blue wing pattern is distinctive. Lakeland fly-fishermen once used the wing feathers for their artficial flies.

Tawny Owl

(Strix aluco)

This thoroughly nocturnal owl is well named. The plumage is tawny-brown above, with a slightly lighter tone beneath. The general brownish tone is varied by darker markings that make it hard to distinguish a daytime-roosting bird from the tree against which it is perched. The dark eyes are set in a large facial disc, which is thought to funnel the sound to the bird's ears. The male owl does most of the hooting and both include in their vocabulary a sharp "kee-wick." This is especially so when there are territorial disputes or when the young of the year are being persuaded to leave.

A few words of warning. Tawny owls are best left alone. Should you come across one or two downy young owls perched on a wall or fence by day, ignore them or you might be attacked by one of the parent owls, which usually strike from behind.

The nest of a pair of tawny owls is usually in a tree-hole, so these birds frequent older, mixed woodland. As you would expect, a tawny owl has sharp eyes and acute hearing, though is inclined when hungry to drop on its prey – usually small mammals – from a perch. The bird is recognised as a predator by small birds, which are inclined to mob it.

Goldcrest

(Regulus regulus)

If you hear a high-pitched call – "see, see, see" – when in a woodland setting, you might confidently look for the goldcrest, the smallest British bird species. Let the calls direct you to the tiny bird which, having short wings and tail, looks dumpy. Apart from a yellow, black-edged crown, on which there is a dab of orange, the male goldcrest is dull-looking, with olive-green above and a

greenish tinge to the lighter underparts. The female lacks the orange touch on the head.

Sometimes the goldcrest will give you time to study it (it is almost as though it is studying *you*) but will soon move off – a diminutive bird with whirring wings. Goldcrests are sometimes found in a mixed company of tits that process through the winter deciduous woods. The bird is mainly associated with coniferous woods, where it makes a delicate hammock-like nest in this sheltered habitat.

Sparrow Hawk

(Accipiter nisus)

The male is dark grey above with reddish or orange wash on the underparts. The (larger) female has a mantle of brownish-grey. This supreme low-level flier has short blunt wings and barred tail. The sounds uttered by a sparrow hawk are pitched high – a series of rapid "kek" sounds. In fact, it relies greatly on the silent approach to its prey, taking its small-bird prey by surprise.

The sparrow hawk, established where there is adequate tree cover, benefited from afforestation with conifers. While the female broods young at a twiggy platform in a larch tree some 14 ft/4m above the ground, the male leaves semi-dressed prey at a "plucking post" from which it is collected by the female, who feeds it to the nestlings. One such post held the remains of redstart, wheatear, pigeon, ring ouzel and mistle thrush.

A pair feeding young in a southern conifer plantation preyed extensively on juvenile starlings. Tissie Fooks, who had a woodland estate in the Rusland Valley, acquired some ornamental doves for a cote beside the house – and lost one bird a day to the local sparrow hawks. This high-speed bird has, in pursuit of prey, been known to crash where there are houses with large windows, front and back, giving the impression of clear space. The bird has either killed itself or been stunned, leaving a dusty impression of its body and wings on the glass.

Woodcock

(Scolopax rusticola)

When a woodcock squats on its nest on the ground in an oak wood, its plumage harmonises with the rich tones round about. One old Lakeland poacher claimed to be able to detect a crouching woodcock by the sparkle in its eye. A large, plump bird, the woodcock has a long bill.

The woodcock is an early nester, laying its eggs in a shallow depression in an oak wood, the eggs resting on nothing more than a few dead leaves. This bird roosts by day and feeds by night, visiting marshy areas where it might probe for food with its long bill, which has a sensitive tip. The bird might therefore eat worms, insect larvae and other invertebrates without actually seeing them.

A bird flying round its nesting territory, following a prescribed route, is said to be roding. The woodcock uses slow wing-beats and is roughly at a height of about 50 ft. The patrolling woodcock periodically gives voice – three grunts and a squeak!

The Lakeland population of woodcock is greatly augmented by Continental birds in winter.

Pheasant

(Phasianus cochicus)

The cock bird, a resplendent figure, with copper-brown body, dark-green head with red wattles and elegantly long tail, may be seen strutting at the side of a road as well as at the fringes of woodland. The female is smaller and browner. The main call of the pheasant is a coarse "kok-kok," used when birds fly noisily to roost in tall trees where they are safe from terrestrial enemies like the fox.

Much of the landscape was modified when, in the 19th century, the shooting of game birds was at the peak of popularity among the landed gentry. A small army of gamekeepers was maintained. Woodland was under-drawn with rhododendrons as game-cover. The ring-necked type of pheasant originated in China.

Gamekeepers used to rear pheasants and keep down any creatures that might prey on them, classifying such creatures as "vermin." Now most pheasants arrive on the estate as poults acquired from game farms, though an appreciable number of pheasants that escape the autumnal guns will nest in the wild. The female sits her clutch of 15 eggs for about 25 days.

Nuthatch

(Sitta europaea)

A ringing call heard in mature woodland, especially beech and oak (which are a common "mix" in Lakeland) announces that a nuthatch is present. When moving on the trunk of a tree, the nuthatch is not a difficult bird to see, being blue-grey above, sandy-brown below, with a white throat and cheeks. A black stripe extends through the eye.

The nuthatch scutters about on the trunk and branches of a tree, the arrangement of its claws allowing it to move adroitly in any direction. A pair of birds nest in a hole which is plastered up until the entrance is of the precise size of the bird, discouraging intruders.

A nuthatch, prime hacker of hazel nuts, beech mast and acorns, tends to lodge one in a crack before breaking it open with its powerful little beak. Examples of woodland favoured by nuthatches are Grasmere and the thin woodland reached by following the shore path east of Friars Crag, Derwentwater.

In winter, nuthatches benefit from the generosity of people living in houses with a woodland setting who maintain bird tables and nurture the birds through spells of grim weather. They have been largely responsible for its numerical increase since the 1960s, when a few nuthatches occurred in the Ambleside and Sedbergh areas. (It is estimated there are in excess of 200 pairs in Cumbria today).

Green Woodpecker

(Picus viridus)

You are more likely to hear the yaffle [laughing call] of the green woodpecker than to have a good close view of the bird. The undulating flight, as it moves from one tree to another, usually in park-like countryside, is distinctive. Close by, this woodpecker is seen to have red on the crown, a dark moustachial stripe, green mantle, grey-green underparts and a yellowish rump.

The green woodpecker is a species of park-like rather than dense woodland. It has a strong association with areas holding nests of wood ants, an example being the Duddon Valley. Ants are scooped up using a long, sticky tongue which emerges from a powerful bill.

Great Spotted Woodpecker

(Dendrocopus major)

This woodpecker is black and white, with red on the under tail coverts. The male bird has a red spot on the neck. In contrast with the highly vocal green woodpecker, both male and female of the great spotted species fancy themselves

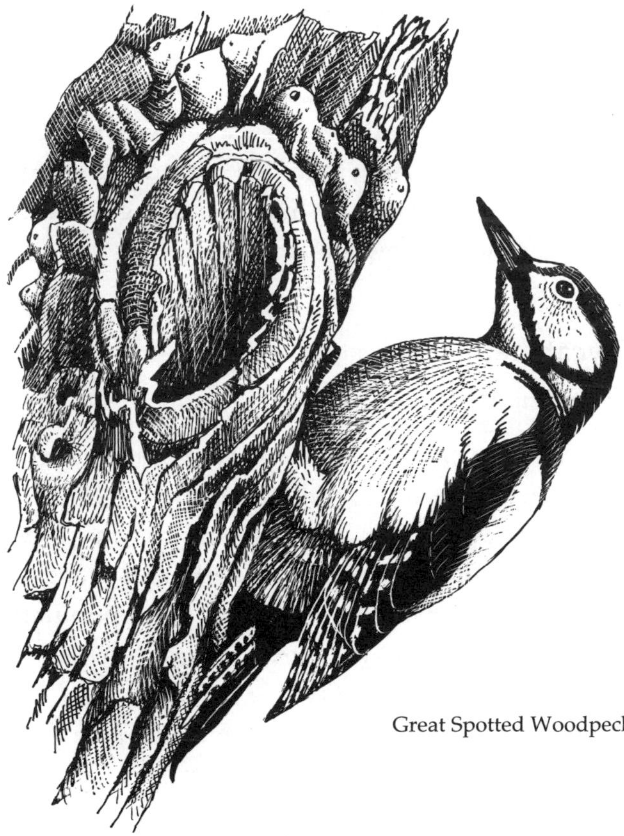

Great Spotted Woodpecker

as percussionists and will "drum" on the hollow branches of trees. It is a call associated with the breeding season.

The great spotted woodpecker, a pied bird which is more conspicuous and widely distributed than the green, is somewhat smaller, being about the size of a starling. It causes great excitement when visiting bird tables in winter.

Winter is the best time to look for the **lesser spotted woodpecker**, for it is then that it might join up with a nomadic group of titmice and fellow travellers such as tree-creeper and goldcrest. To see a lesser spotted woodpecker is an occasion for rejoicing. This sparrow-sized bird spends most of its time in the tree canopy. When the leaves unfurl in spring, seeing the bird is especially difficult. Wooded areas beside the River Kent and Leighton Moss are two areas where this elusive bird has been recorded.

The lesser spotted woodpecker has a fairly long "drumming" season, extending from February until the second half of April. Its drumming is scarcely detectable by humans, being little more than the sound made by a wind-blown tree.

Pied Flycatcher

(Ficedula hypoleuca)

The male bird has an attractive black and white plumage; the somewhat drab female is grey-brown above, with a light-coloured wing bar.

The pied flycatcher arrives in mid-May and is with us until September. Its preference is for damp deciduous woods, which means that Lakeland is a most suitable habitat. The population has risen through the introduction of nest box schemes; where boxes are provided, the species is found nesting at over 1,200 ft.

The **spotted flycatcher**, which is the slightly larger bird, is more widespread and watchable. Both sexes look alike, being basically grey-brown above, paler beneath. Darker spots and streaks adorn the plumage. The spotted is often seen near the haunts of humankind and takes readily to nest boxes. A perching bird leaps out to intercept passing insects.

Chaffinch

(Fringilla coelebs)

Local names: Scobby, Scoppy

If you hear a cheerful "pink, pink" during a woodland walk, then you are in the company of the chaffinch. The cock chaffinch is a bobby-dazzler in its summer plumage, which features a blue-grey crown and nape, black forehead, pink breast and chestnut mantle. The wings are brown, enlivened by yellowish wing bars. There is white on the shoulders and white flanks the dark tail. The female is smaller and paler.

This common woodland bird is confiding where it is regularly fed, as at rural refreshment vans, one of many examples being the Devil's Bridge at Kirkby Lonsdale. Wintering flocks favour the mild south-west corner of Lakeland.

Redstart

(Phoenicurus phoenicurus)

Local name: Firetail

The most conspicuous feature of this summer visitor to old woodland – a bird which has the general appearance and stance of a robin – is the "firey tail," which is bright orange. Redstarts flick their tails, as though trying to shake them off. The cock redstart is a showy bird, with a black face and throat, grey upperparts, chestnutty breast and flanks. The female, which has the main nesting duties, is grey-brown above and a buffish tone beneath.

The redstart, a shy bird, nests in holes in trees, in walls or buildings.

Redstart

Among its Lakeland haunts are the woods at the back of Brothers Water, Grizedale Forest and the older timbered areas of the Windermere area.

Tree Creeper

(Certhia familiaris)

Streaky-brown above, white underneath, with light eye stripe and wing bars. The tree creeper resembles a little mouse as it moves erratically up the trunk of a tree, propping itself with stiffened tail feathers as it probes for insect food in the bark using a needle-thin downcurved beak.

Notice how it begins its food-hunting close to the base of a tree, climbing spirally and then flying to the base of the next tree. It has been discovered that some tree-creepers have a winter roost in a saucer-like depression made in the soft bark of the tree popularly known as the Wellingtonia. The nest is usually placed behind a piece of loose bark.

Willow Warbler

(Phylloscopus trochilus)

Olive-green above, faintly yellow and white beneath, the willow warbler is a bird to cheer us up when it arrives in April, its relatively long wings having carried it from wintering areas to the south of the Sahara.

At least, from the identification point of view, the plumage is contrasty, the bird having a clear white "eyebrow" and a wistful song that might be quickly memorised, being an oft-repeated ditty that runs down the scale.

This species might be confused visually with the **chiffchaff**, which has a darker body, helpfully calls its name repeatedly and is inclined to be at the woodland edge rather than among the trees.

Wood Warbler

(Phylloscopus sibilatrix)

Garden Warbler

(Sylvia borin)

The so-called leaf warblers, which are summer visitors, are generally unobtrusive in their manner and plumage. That of the wood warbler is relatively bright, with a green back and yellow throat and upper breast. The garden warbler has no special features to help in identification. It's the classic "small brown job."

Firstly, chose the right location. The wood warbler's preference is for sessile oakwoods and beechwoods (which have hardly any understorey). At the beginning of the century, Miss M L Armitt found wood warblers were "extremely common" in the oakwoods of the Ambleside-Grasmere area, but this is no longer the case. The garden warbler seeks out woodland or areas of scrub.

A great help in identifying birds is by their calls. Buy or borrow a recording of bird songs and memorise those of the elusive warblers.

The call of the wood warbler is a protracted whistle and, when in song, it renders what has been described as "a shivering trill." When singing, it sometimes flits, with shimmering wings, from one branch to another, moving horizontally.

The call of the garden warbler is harsh and grating, though it does manage from somewhere among dense foliage to produce a bubbling song.

As a matter of interest, the wood warbler nests on the ground, quite often in the vegetation beside a fallen tree. The garden warbler seeks out a low situation, invariably among a tangle of bramble or patch of nettles.

Whinchat

(Saxicola rubetra)

Stonechat

(Saxicola torquata)

These birds like to observe the world from a high perch. Each bird has darkish upperparts with reddish-orange at the breast. Each has a white wing patch. The whinchat, smaller and daintier than its cousin, is identifiable by having a white strip above and below the eye. The stonechat has a strip of white at the neck that contrasts markedly with a black crown.

The whinchat is a summer visitor and the stonechat a resident. They favour coastal haunts, where the land is roughish and there are patches of gorse. Inland, their ranges tend to overlap on the shrubby edges of moorland.

Crossbill

(Loxia curvirostra)

Look for this species in coniferous areas. Frustratingly, it spends most of its time in the canopy. The bird is a finch with a big head and crossed mandibles. The male is dull red, the female mainly green. The call is a loud "jip-jip."

A useful tip is to look in the chosen conifer wood for a pool or even a puddle. The crossbill, feeding exclusively on conifer seeds, must regularly slack its thirst.

The birds begin nesting in winter as pine seeds ripen. Two Lakeland haunts are Grizedale Forest and lakeside woods near Coniston.

Lakes and Streams

When the last phase of the Ice Age drew to a close, all the lakes were presumably in much the same condition. They have been changing ever since, some more rapidly than others. Wastwater and Ennerdale, in the north west of Lakeland, have changed least. Esthwaite Lake, between Coniston Water and Windermere, is the most changed lake. Almost half its drainage area is cultivated, as opposed to only about five per cent at Wastwater.

Waterfowl are attracted to shallow and sheltered bays, as by Windermere. Generally, it is the head of a lake and the place where the water outflows that provide most interest to bird-watchers. An example is Coniston Water, where birds tend to congregate mostly at the Nibthwaite end.

Manchester Waterworks plugged a little valley called Mardale and transformed two relatively small lakes into a large reservoir known as Haweswater. A Lakeland poet, Norman Nicholson, commenting on the transformation, said that such work meant that the big hills now stand up to their waists in cold water. Manchester also took over the neighbouring Wet Sleddale; the reservoirs are inter-related, a tunnel being driven through the fell. The Haweswater area, where the ornithological interests are attended to by the RSPB, has a wide range of bird-life, from goldcrest to golden eagle.

A prime area for waterfowl is Leighton Moss, which lies in a pleasant wooded valley among limestone hills near Silverdale. The Moss is a reserve of the RSPB. Here are well-maintained facilities. Firm paths lead between reed beds that are enlivened in spring by yellow iris. Hides overlook stretches of open water.

Eric Simms, in *A Natural History of Britain and Ireland* (1979), mentioned the bitterns that "boom in their lugubrious bovine way from mid-January to June and seem to be particularly stimulated by the sound of diesel locomotives on the nearby railway line." At Leighton Moss, reed warblers chatter and water rails squeal and grunt.

Mute Swan

(Cygnus olor)

Our largest bird is familiar to all, being found on rivers as well as lakes and on many ornamental waters. Notice the orange and black bill with an adjacent dark knob. Also observe that, when swimming, the mute swan holds its neck in an S-curve.

For the closest views of mute swans, go to the promenade at Bowness Bay in summer. Swans may be seen walking among a host of visitors.

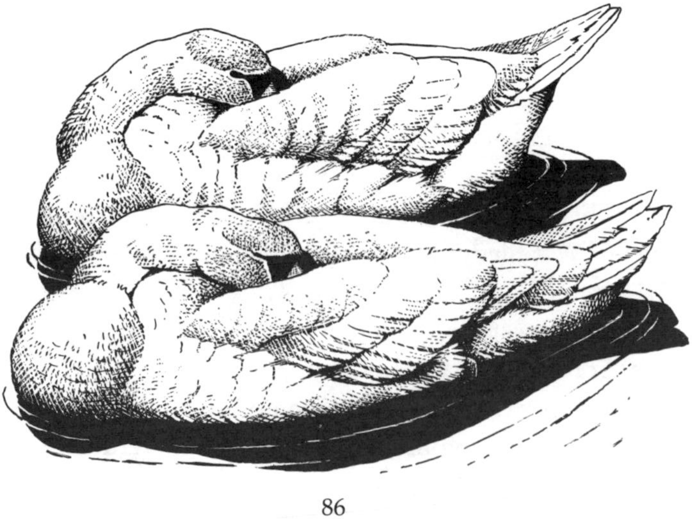

Whooper Swan

(Cygnus cygnus)

Bewick's Swan

(Cygnus columbianus)

A winter visitor, the whooper swan is superficially like the mute swan but has a yellow bill tipped with black. The yellow extends so far forward, the shape is that of a wedge. The whooper holds its neck erect and frequently utters crooning and bugling contact calls. Bewick's swan, if seen in the company of whoopers, will be found to be smaller and with a shorter neck. The flight calls sound at times like that made by a pack of hounds. A whooper swan weighs up to 24 lb with Bewick's tipping the scales at 11 lb - 17 lb.

Icelandic "whoopers" cross the North Atlantic to Scotland, cruising at an elevation of between 2,000 ft and 4,000 ft and a speed of up to 70 miles an hour. They accomplish the non-stop flight in about 16 hours. Britain, in a temperate area, is an important wintering location.

Whooper swans were once seen regularly on a variety of lakes, especially Elterwater (the name means "swan lake"), Grasmere and Rydal. Family parties include the dusky young of the year. Nowadays, when vast numbers of wintering whooper swans are enticed by regular feeding to reserves at Caerlaverock (north of Solway) and Martin Mere (Lancashire), we have fewer sightings. The largest concentration of migratory swans, some 1,500 birds, occurs at the Ouse Washes, in the east.

Bewick's swan *(Cygnus columbianus)*, being a smaller relative of the whooper, is almost goose-like in appearance and nests in Arctic Siberia, this being at a higher latitude than the regions favoured by the whooper swan. Incidentally, Bewick's swan is named after the celebrated Northumbrian bird-engraver. The migratory journey to wintering grounds covers 2,500 miles and is accomplished in stages over two months.

Greylag

(Anser anser)

A heavy goose, greyish-brown in colour with a large orange bill and pink legs. The greylag was the principal ancestor of our domestic goose. The call is farmyardy – "ang-ang-ang."

The greylag's return to England as a nesting species, after about two centuries, began with a rearing scheme at The Hawes reserve near Millom. Here, in 1961, the eggs of greylags of Scottish origin were hatched out under foster geese. Three pairs of greylags nested in the wild at Coniston Water in 1963. Henceforth, the spread of greylags was fairly rapid. The species now nests widely in the Lake District.

Derwentwater has proved popular with greylags, which might be seen grazing on grassland adjacent to the path leading from Keswick to Friars Crag – though not many people notice their grey-brown forms or they take them to be domestic stock. A wintering flock of about 200 birds ranges from Windermere to Grasmere.

A large flock of greylags, many of them from Iceland, musters each winter in the Eden Valley, roosting at Watersmeet (where the Eamont joins the Eden). The estate is private but birds can usually be overlooked from the road between Langwathby and Culgaith. Grazing birds are observed at various places in the district, including land beside the main Appleby-Penrith road where it is joined by the road from Culgaith.

Cormorant

(Phalacrocorax carbo)

The dark bird, lying long and low in the water, is almost certainly a cormorant. Look at the head and neck, which give it a strong reptillian appearance. In flight, the bird moves quickly, though on wings that beat relatively slowly. When perched on a tall lakeside tree, the cormorant holds out its wings and then resembles a Germanic emblem. The bird is said to be drying its wings but might equally well be relaxing its muscles after a heavy meal.

The cormorant, formerly associated with the sea-coast, is now commonly seen inland, on lakes and rivers, where it uses its considerable fishing skills to the detriment of the local fisheries.

Tree-roosting parties of cormorants might be seen by Windermere and on islets in Coniston Water and Haweswater. Cormorants have been seen flying over High Street in the evening before descending to roost in trees at the southern end of Haweswater.

Kingfisher

(Alcedo atthis)

When a kingfisher perches among foliage at the side of a river or beck, the orange breast breaks up the outline of the bird. Only when it flies, fast and low, is the celebrated electric-blue plumage apparent. Overall, the kingfisher is blue-grey above and orange beneath. Notice (if there is time) the white on the side of the neck and the throat.

Mild winters and pollution prevention measures keep the kingfisher population relatively high. When water is crusted with ice, the birds cannot feed and must either migrate downriver or die.

A kingfisher patiently sits on the trailing bough of a tree, scanning the water for small-fish prey. If disturbed, it flies fast and low over the water. Undisturbed, a hungry bird either hovers above the water or plunges from a nearby perch, keeping its wings close to its side. Underwater, having grasped a minnow, it uses its wings vigorously to regain the surface. The leap from the water is possible through a powerful downbeat. The bird returns to its perch. Any fish food is swallowed head first.

The nest is in a chamber at the end of a hole driven in an earthen bank. The parent birds soon make it clear to their young that they must move on and find their own territories, which can be long but little wider than the watercourse that provides them with food. A young kingfisher must learn to fish quickly, for it must soon quit the home territory for a stretch of its own.

Common Sandpiper

(Actitis hypeleucos)

Local name: Willie Liltie

This little wading bird is brown above, white beneath, with a white notch at the shoulder. It is forever bobbing its rear end, as though using up surplus energy. When in low, level flight, it uses flickering, shallow wingbeats inter-

spersed with short glides. The bird has a tittering flight call – "see-wee-wee."

The common sandpiper winters in West Africa, returning to its Lakeland nesting haunts in late April or early May. A species found mainly in northern and western Britain has its Lakeland nesting places beside lakes, reservoirs, tarns and streams up to about 1,500 ft. In popular areas, there is unwitting disturbance by holidaymakers.

This sandpiper feeds among pebbles, dining on beetles and insects. The late start to the nesting season is compensated by a latish departure (September) to the African wintering haunts.

Sand Martin

(Riparia riparia)

Brown above, white beneath, with a brown band across the breast – these are the basic details of the plumage of a small, slim member of the swallow tribe. The wings are quite short, the fork in the tail much less pronounced than that of the swallow.

The sand martin arrives quite early and soon the air around a selected nesting area, such as a riverbank beside a river, the Kent or Eden, seems half full of flickering brownish forms. The nest is at the end of a burrow. Sandpits may be colonised.

The sand martin's method of taking insects when on the wing has lured at least one bird to take the artificial fly cast by an angler. The species cheerfully survives, though river spates may sometimes seriously impede a season's nesting programme.

Grey Heron

(Ardea cinerea)

Local names: Heronsue or Crane

This lanky, grey-and-white bird, a master of inactivity, has been confused for a waterside post as it keeps watch for fish food. It is easily overlooked. In flight, the bird looks immense but moves adroitly in confined areas between

tree branches as it leaves the river. At close quarters, the heron is seen to have black eyebrows (they develop into a headcrest).

Nesting is colonial, at the tops of high trees. There is a famous heronry near Dallam Tower, an area handy for fishing in the Kent estuary. Herons nested on conifers growing on an island in Rydal Water in the 1820s. Christopher North wrote that "the heronry on the high pine trees of the island connects the scene with the ancient park of Rydal."

Harriet Martineau, a distinguished Victorian writer who settled at Ambleside, was impressed by "the grey bird" that might be seen "perched upon a tree near its nest, or fishing in the shallows of its island home." Rather more than 40 years later, the heronry was deserted, The birds had moved to a larch plantation, west of the lake.

Shoveler

(Anas clypeata)

Local name: Spoonbill

This smallish, dabbling duck has a large, shovel-shaped bill and at first glance looks as though it might tip up! Look for the chestnut-red belly and flanks.

Tufted Duck, Goldeneye and Shoveler

The shoveler frequents rich shallow waters, including the meres at Leighton Moss, but has been reported from larger stretches of water such as the reservoirs at Haweswater and in Wet Sleddale near Shap.

The beak that looks so awkward is in fact a notable means whereby the bird can dine on miniscule food-items. The beak broadens at the tip. A great volume of water is admitted and food is filtered out by hair-like projections.

Coot

(Fulica atra)

Local name: Lake Hen

The coot, dark and duck-like, is a member of the rail family, to which the waterhen, another bird of quiet waters, belongs. Notice on the coot the white frontal shield – hence the old saying "as bald as a coot." In clear water or when the bird is on land, it will be seen that the feet are not webbed. The toes of the coot are lobed. This bird has a ringing call and, when alarmed, utters a sudden explosive sound, like an avian sneeze.

The coot likes open water, and in the shallows dines on aquatic plants. It is perhaps the most numerous duck on Windermere in winter. This bird has an aggressive disposition towards other water birds.

The nest is capable of floating but is well-tethered to the branch of a tree where it overhangs the water. Young coot are covered in black down.

Tufted Duck

(Aythya fuligula)

As with many species of ducks, the appearance of the drake is markedly different from that of the duck. In this case, the male has a pied plumage, with black above and white below. Notice a drooping headcrest. The female has a dark-brown plumage.

A common duck, it is frequently seen on Windermere (where, in November 1979, no less than 346 birds were counted). The tufted duck is not particularly shy and is found on ornamental waters, such as lakes in parks.

Goldeneye

(Bucephala clangula)

Local name: Golding (Westmorland)

This small black-and-white diving duck has a high-peaked head and a conspicuous large white spot at the base of the bill.

A bird that nests in thick wooded countryside, in areas where the new-hatched ducklings might have to undertake a long walk to water, is in winter mainly a marine creature. Standing water in Lakeland does attract an appreciable number.

The scientific name "clangula" implies that the bird is noisy, which is not exactly the case, though in flight its wings produce what has been described as a "singing" sound.

Great Crested Grebe

(Podiceps cristatus)

In its breeding plumage, the great crested grebe acquires some showy head adornments, known as tippets. These chestnut feathers shade to black at the tips. They were once coveted by milliners to adorn the hats of society ladies. In winter, the great-crested grebe looks very ordinary, having dark-grey upperparts and white underparts.

This, the largest of the grebes found in home waters, nests on several of the smaller lakes and some suitable tarns. Reed-edged Esthwaite Water is ideal for the species, though it is less numerous here than it was.

The spring display of grebes in their exotic nuptial plumage brings to Lakeland a touch of Oriental splendour. Being similar in appearance, each plays a part in a complicated rite that leads to pair-bonding.

The **little grebe**, also known as the dabchick, is a stubby little bird that has the buoyancy and something of the appearance of a cork. Notice the chestnut tinge of the throat, cheeks and forehead, which contrasts with a black border. The chestnut coloration is lost in winter, when the bird looks extremely plain.

Red-breasted Merganser

(Mergus serrator)

This species is one of the "sawbills," so called because of the serrations on the bill that enable it to grasp slippery fish prey. The merganser is smaller and slimmer than another familiar "sawbill," namely the goosander. The male bird has a large crest but goes into eclipse [moult] from May onwards. The chestnut breast merges into black shoulders. The flanks are grey. The female is mostly grey with a gingery-coloured head.

Merganser is an English word coined in the 16th century from the Latin for "diving goose." For long a breeder in Scotland, it was first noted as breeding in England in 1950 and the southward expansion continues. With the goosander, it is unloved by anglers, being a prime competitor for trout.

Goosander

Mergus Merganser
Local name: Gravel Duck

The male, a most handsome bird, sports a large head, of greenish hue, a black back, white breasts and flanks. The bill and legs are red. The female has a reddish-brown head, pearl-grey back and slightly duller white undersides. The headcrest, a characteristic of each sex, sometimes lies so flat it is inconspicuous.

The goosander, big and powerful, as you might see if it is keeping its place on a river in spate, is a recent colonist, having bred in England since 1941. It is attracted more by fresh than salt water, the reverse of the situation with its cousin, the red-breasted merganser.

There was excitement in 1971 when a pair of goosanders had a brood of 10 on Haweswater. That year, a goosander with nine young was seen on Ullswater. Other early nesting haunts were Wet Sleddale reservoir, Angle Tarn and Brothers Water. The species expanded its range southwards at a dramatic rate. Breeding takes place mainly on upland rivers, with nests made in holes in riverside trees and banks.

Dipper

(Cinclus cinclus)
Local name: Bessy Ducker

Seen at close quarters, and in good light, the dipper has a plumage of chocolate brown with a prominent white bib. In poor light, the bird appears black but the bill is still conspicuous. Notice its chubby appearance and small tail. The bird frequently bobs while standing on a water-washed boulder. When feeding, it either walks into the water or dives with a plop, dining on aquatic insects, crustaceans and molluscs, also small fish.

The Lakeland name, Bessy Ducker, relates to a Norse word, *dukke,* meaning "to dip or dive." The dipper frequents Lakeland becks and

Dipper

larger watercourses that flow fast and clear and, as related, finds its food on the bed. If you see a bird "flying" underwater, which is possible, such is the clarity of our rivers, notice how it has a silvery appearance from air trapped in its plumage.

The highest density of dippers is in the peripheral areas of the Lake District. Hill birds may nest later than those on the lower reaches. W R Philipson, in a delightful book on Lakeland bird life, published in 1948, mentioned when he was dipper-watching by Goldrill Beck he was entranced by the fortitude of the dipper.

Philipson had heard it singing a few days before Christmas "and at the turn of the year, after snow and cold winds, he sang his song [an attractive warbling] again. But a north-country bird that will lay its eggs in March, even with snow on the ground, may be expected to sing under all conditions."

Grey Wagtail

(Motacilla cinerea)

This slim and elegant riverside bird, which is usually seen in the haunts of dippers, is tinted blue-grey above, with a yellowish rump and bright yellow underparts. The cock bird has a black throat when in breeding plumage.

Like the dipper, the grey wagtail often perches on boulders in midstream, but instead of "bobbing" the wagtail lives up to its name. It dines on a variety of insect life and thus does not lead the aquatic life known to the dipper.

A bird of clear, fast-flowing streams, the grey wagtail is most commonly found where watercourses are broader and their banks are lined by trees. Most birds leave Lakeland after the nesting season but a few winter on the lower reaches of the main rivers.

The **yellow wagtail**, a summer visitor, has a relatively short tail. This is a bird of damp meadows. One of its Lakeland haunts is at the head of Bassenthwaite Lake.

On the Coast

Norman Nicholson collected a series of poems under the title *Sea to the West*. He lived at Millom, a curious little 19th century town built beside rich deposits of iron ore, close to marsh and mudflat. Those who climb the high fells of Lakeland in clear weather cannot fail to be aware of the coast. Far to the west, sands gleam and there is a shimmer on the tide as it flows, reputedly with the speed of a good horse.

Northwards is Solway and, beyond, the blue hills of Scotland. Solway Firth is a major winter resort of waders, ducks and geese. On the English shore, between Rockcliffe and Grune Point, are vast expanses of salt marshes, where geese are numbered by the thousand. The pink-footed geese nested in Iceland. The smaller barnacle goose, which are counted among the black geese, have flown in stages from their nesting grounds in Spitzbergen.

Notice, when the sky seems half full of geese, how many of them are in chevron formation, forming huge letter Vs. It is an energy-saving device, the wingbeats of one goose creating a slight upward air current that benefits the following bird. The hard work is performed by the leader. It is fascinating to see how periodically there is a change of leader so that one bird is not working all the time at full stretch.

The so-called grey geese, which include the pink-foots and greylags, may be too high for the fine points of plumage to be noticed. Listen to their calling, that of the pink-footed geese being a fairly light *wink, wink* and the greylag having a farmyardy sound. When in flight, the pink-foots are usually more evenly spaced than are the larger greylags.

Down the west coast of Cumbria you will surely wish to walk on the path across the headland just north of St Bees – a headland of redstone cliffs with generous ledges for nesting auks and gulls. Ravenglass stands near where three rivers meet and blend their cold, clear water with the tawny swirl of the tides. In Morecambe Bay are several former islands, now tethered to the mainland, where the bird life is profuse and varied.

Ann Ratcliffe described in the 18th century how she made the crossing of Morecambe Bay from Hest Bank to the Cartmel shore. Her destination was Grange, later to be known as Grange-over-Sands. "The tide was ebbing fast from our wheels, and its low murmur was interrupted, first, only by the shrill small cry of seagulls, unseen, whose hovering flight could be traced by the sound, near an island that began to dawn through the mist, and, then, by the hoarser croaking of sea-geese."

Morecambe Bay, part land, part sea, is one of the most important region for waders in Europe. The sands are relatively undisturbed and attract large numbers of birds to an area rich in invertebrate life. The flats are rich in bivalves, shrimps, marine worms and sandhoppers. Mussels in plenty adorn the skeers and sustain the eiders that, hereabouts, are at their most southerly breeding area on the west coast.

Hest Bank, where in pre-railway days there was a busy inter-tide traffic across the Sands, is now well developed, but beyond the marshland in winter you might see the packed bodies of waders, including dunlin and knot, grey and white, waiting – as did the travellers of old – for the turn of the tide. Old names for the dapper little dunlin were "purr" or "sea-mouse." The knot was once known to the residents of Walney Island as "sea-grey."

The air above Morecambe Bay may suddenly seem half full of parties of oystercatchers, displaced by rushing water from their feeding grounds lower down the huge tidal inlet. At other times, godwit and curlew stalk the tideline. In July, you might see a small "curlew" with a whitish eye stripe and a tittering call. This is a whimbrel on passage to southern wintering grounds. The air holds the whistle of wigeon and you may hear the laughing call of a shelduck. Bird traffic is incessant in spring, when a northward migration is occurring. The ringed plovers that trip over the wet mud, stopping now and again to pick up oddments of food, may be refuelling for a flight to Greenland.

Remember that with ducks you will see some tatty specimens at the end of the breeding season when their plumage is in the stage known as "eclipse" and the birds are temporarily flightless. The bright eider drake is transformed by the moult to a bird that is sooty-black.

Pink-footed Goose

(Anser brachyrhynchus)

Compared with the greylag, the pink-foot has a small dark brown head, a short, thickish neck and pale grey forewings. The relatively short bill is pink, with a black tip, and as the bird's name implies, the legs are pink.

The pinkfoot nests in central Iceland, with a quite small population in eastern Greenland. The migration of many thousands of birds to winter quarters is across hundreds of miles of the uneasy North Atlantic. Solway is a great "marshalling yard" from which geese fly to other areas, notably Martin Mere in Lancashire.

Oystercatcher

(Haematopus ostralegus)

Local name: Sea Pie

Look for a large black and white wader with a long, orange bill, the size and colour reminding older people of a stick of sealing wax. The bird is black above and on the throat, white beneath. It has pink legs. Anyone who has seen an oystercatcher close up, as from a hide on South Walney at high tide, will have noticed the white circlet round a red eye. An excitable bird, the oystercatcher calls shrilly as it circles when disturbed at the nest, the eggs being laid in a depression in shingle or, in a few cases, on shingle beds or fields beside rivers.

The Cumbrian coast has a goodly number of nesting pairs and over the past few decades oystercatchers have taken to nesting by river systems far inland. The shingle beds of the Eden are an easterly example.

Shelduck

Morecambe Bay is a major wintering ground for oystercatchers, immigration from the Continent being noted. The contact call is a shrill *kleep, kleep*. With a reduction in the size of the cockle beds, the birds have spent more time feeding inland.

Shelduck

(Tadorna tadorna)

Local name: Skelduck (Solway)

This goose-like duck is dark above, white below. The darkness is a glossy green, though it will look black in dull light. There is black along the edges of the wings. Notice the tip-tilted red beak. A chestnut band crosses the breast. The male shelduck is inclined to whistle and the female to quack.

At low tide, the muddy areas bear the marks of shelduck, both the footprints and impressions left by the beak when feeding. The shelduck feeds on small molluscs, the commonest, *hydrobia,* living just under the surface. To collect food, the bird waddles slowly across an expanse of wet mud, its beak just buried, and makes scything movements of its head. During this process, the sensitive tip is detecting the molluscs, which are drawn in.

At other times, a shelduck might be seen stamping on mud, which presumably makes it more fluid or indeed actually draws food to the surface. The process of agitating the sand or mud was known to the fishermen of the Bay who operated at low tide and, when collecting cockles, used Jumbo, a wooden device with a broad base board to reveal the whereabouts of the shellfish which, being brought to the surface, were then harvested using a handfork known as a *kraam*.

The shelduck is a burrow-nesting species and when the youngsters appear and are led towards the sea by the parents they are striped, like humbugs. Shelduck nesting along the coastal edge of Lakeland once had a moult migration eastwards across the Pennines and the North Sea to the Heligoland Bight, off the German coast. Most adult shelduck departed in late July and returned, with their new plumage gleaming, in October. The adults that remained in our country were those left attending to large creches of juvenile birds.

Increasing numbers of shelduck now summer in the home areas, frequenting the river estuaries during the flightless period. One notable gathering place is an island between the Mersey and the Manchester Ship Canal. Some of the birds of Cumbrian origin are believed to moult in the West Country.

Eider

(Smateria mollissima)

The eider drake reverses the normal plumage pattern. In the breeding season it is white above, dark below. Notice how the powerful beak gives the bird a long straight forehead. There is a faint green hue to the nape. The drake has a soft, crooning call – "ooOOoo." The eider duck is overall brown but at close-range, the brown is seen to have a delicate pattern of darker marks. She sits tight on her ground nest, looking like a feathered tea-cosy.

South Walney is the place to visit to see eiders. Early in the year, there are many drakes, yet once the mating time is over they tend to move off, further out, where they moult, subsisting on the mussel-beds, their powerful beaks cracking open the shells.

The footpaths on the South Walney reserve pass fairly close to sitting birds. The restless tide is usually dotted with adult birds and, in season, with the dark, fluffy ducklings which, in the form of creches, are attended to by several ducks. They are quick to see danger from hungry gulls.

Eider

Redshank

(Tringa totanus)

Grey-brown, with moderately long orange-red legs and a black-tipped bill with red at the base. In flight, notice white on the back and upper rump.

The redshank is a small wader with a loud voice – *teu-hu-hu.* It nests in damp meadows, a habitat which has become quite scarce in recent times when drainage and re-seeding have changed their nature. In winter, the redshank is seen almost everywhere in estuaries at low tide. It is easily disturbed and when alarmed calls so shrilly and quickly it might be proclaiming the end of the world.

The larger and rarer **greenshank** is brownish-grey and white with long legs faintly tinged green and a longish, slightly uptilted bill. The bird is a regular passage migrant at such places as Sunbiggin Tarn, Leven and Kent estuaries and Leighton Moss. A small number of greenshanks winters on South Walney. The bird is known as the "titterel" from its call when taking flight. The sound is a quick, ringing whistle.

Where to Watch Birds

A visit to Brockhole, the National Park Centre that is situated just north of Windermere, will through exhibitions, lectures and publications give a stranger to the Lake District a good grounding on landscape and wildlife. Cumbria Wildlife Trust, which has its headquarters at Brockhole, publishes details of its many nature reserves. The initials RSPB stand for the Royal Society for the Protection of Birds, the headquarters of which are at Sandy, Bedfordshire.

The following list provides a brief introduction to a range of Lakeland habitats especially favoured by bird life. Local inquiries will fill in the details. For a modest outlay, acquire four Ordnance Survey (Outdoor Leisure) maps for the Lake District. A prime source of information is *Where to Watch birds in Cumbria, Lancashire and Cheshire,* by Jonathan Guest and Malcolm Hutcheson (published by Christopher Helm, second edition 1997).

Acorn Bank. National Trust property near Culgaith, in the Eden Valley. A red sandstone manor house and herb garden have an oak woodland setting. The house is not open to view, but visitors are welcome to follow some local walks in the season from April to October. The birds to be seen include pied flycatcher (otherwise uncommon in the Eden Valley), woodpeckers, redstart. By the river are goosander, kingfisher, dipper and grey wagtail.

Ambleside. A nature trail leads through Skelghyll Wood. Birds to be seen include jay, buzzard, carrion crow, woodcock, tree-creeper, goldcrest, warblers.

Arnside Knott. (521ft). Car park. A nature trail begins at the mountain indicator. Wren, robin, tit family, goldcrest, tree-creeper, bullfinch, chiffchaff, willow warbler and blackcap. Meadow pipit and yellow hammer frequent open areas. Wooded places hold green and great spotted woodpeckers, tawny owl, jay and woodcock.

Bassenthwaite Lake (fourth largest lake, having a length of four miles). Follow the A66 trunk road north of Keswick to where it runs close (in places actually over) the lake. Skiddaw (locally Skidder) forms a dramatic backdrop. Bassenthwaite Lake is said to be the only lake in the district (other lakes have the suffix –mere or –water). Marked parking places.

At the southern end is Braithwaite Bog, the most extensive fen in Lakeland. Just below Blackstock Point, on the western shore, is a public hide overlooking the Bog. The terrain is varied and so is the bird life, taking in sparrow hawk, buzzard, short-eared owl. Water rails may be heard if not actually seen. Look out for yellow wagtail and listen for sedge and grasshopper warblers.

Summer days in wooded areas near the lake are heady with the songs of chiff chaff and willow warbler. Also present are buzzard, sparrowhawk, wren, robin, five species of tit, treecreeper and goldcrest. Wintering birds include large flocks of duck, coot, mallard, goldeneye, pochard, red-breasted merganser, goosander, great-crested and little grebes. Cormorants may be present. Bassenthwaite Lake has a large gull roost, the species being mainly common and black-headed gulls.

Brothers Water (near the foot of the northern end of Kirkstone Pass and not far from the village of Hartsop). Handy car park near northern end of Brothers Water, which is small and shallow, with damp land to the north and bog and reed-bed to the south. The lake is fed by Dovedale Beck (from the south-west). Dovedale is a resort of ravens. The clear, fast-moving beck suits the dipper.

Follow a footpath on the western shore for extensive views of the lake and its birds. In spring, these include common sandpiper, yellow wagtail and reed bunting, tufted duck, heron and little grebe (also known as the dabchick). Waterfowl visiting Brothers Water in winter include greylag goose, wigeon and goldeneye. Scan the reed beds for siskin and redpoll. Low Wood, which rises from the western shore, is the haunt of buzzard, green woodpecker, nuthatch and tree creeper.

Borrowdale. This scenic valley, south of Keswick, is a microcosm of Lakeland. Here are high fells, tarns, and "hanging" woods. The route from Keswick runs close by Derwentwater, where there is a car park. Greylag geese are among the more prominent of the birds. At the dale-head, around Seathwaite look for ravens. Dipper and grey wagtail inhabit the beck. Snipe may be flushed from damp areas. Fellside woods, being deciduous, hold pied flycatcher, green and great spotted woodpeckers, redstart and woodcock.

Buttermere, Crummock Water, Loweswater. Reached from the Keswick area either through Borrowdale or Newlands Valley. Each road includes a steep pass, that from Borrowdale being Honister Pass and the high spot of the other route being Newlands Hause. Such roads do introduce the visitor to high fell country without physical effort!

Dominating the Buttermere valley are shapely fells – Melbreak, Grasmoor, Red Pike, High Stile. The lake birds include greylag, king-fisher, heron and sandpiper. In winter, look out for swans and also rafts of waterfowl, notably pochard.

Coniston Water. (5½ miles/9.7 km). Approach from Ambleside, via Skelwith Bridge or along a road beginning near Hawkshead, in which case you can delay the approach to Coniston Water by first using a loop road (one-way traffic) that takes you to Tarn Hows (large car park). The best bird-watching is at either end where the water is shal-low and sheltered, though by following a narrow road along the wood-ed eastern side you will see, about half way down, an islet with pine trees (Fir Island) where cormorants roost.

Coniston Water has resident Canada geese and greylags. The lake is good for wintering waterfowl, the species including teal, wigeon, tufted duck, goldeneye and pochard. A winter gull roost consists mainly of common and black-headed gulls. In the woods near Coniston Hall and the boat landing, you stand a reasonable chance of seeing the elusive hawfinch, which is locally common. A screech from the woods indicates the presence of a jay. The wee birds in the trees include crossbill, siskin and redpoll.

Derwentwater. Follow the short Friars Crag Walk from a car park for views (in winter) of mallard, coot, black-headed gull, pochard, tufted duck, goldeneye and heron. Cormorants might be seen diving for fish. Greylags are locally quite numerous, nesting in the area and forming a quite large feeding and roosting flock in the off-season. In the local woods are great spotted woodpeckers, chaffinches and wrens. Wood pigeons converge on local woodland in late autumn for acorns and beech mast.

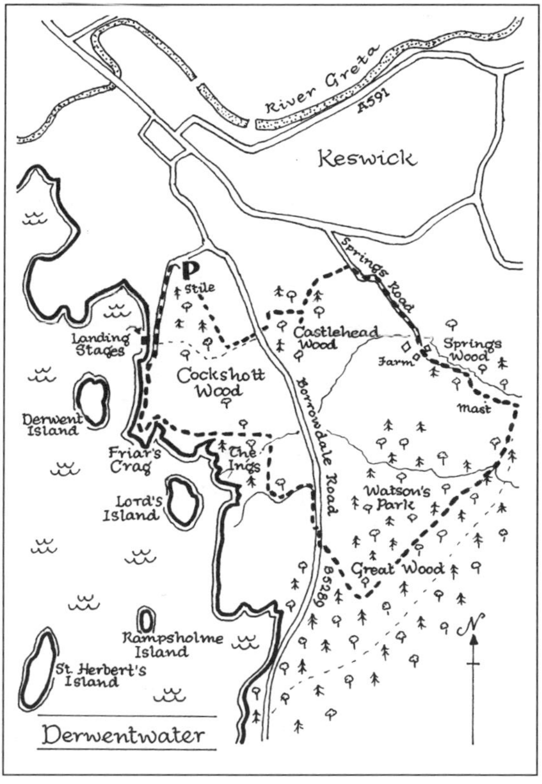

Drigg Dunes Nature Reserve (583 acres). Permits from Cumbria County Council give access to a reserve that is situated just across the estuary from Ravenglass. There is a resident warden. Drigg village is reached using the B5344 from Holmrook.

The estuary is where three rivers – Irt, Mite and Esk – blend their waters between sand dunes. Across the mouth of the estuary are Eskmeals dune system (once used for testing big guns and now noted for its flowers and natterjack toads). Eskmeals, approached from south of the Esk, where a parking area will be found, is administered by the Cumbria Wildlife Trust and is wardened. A permit for entry can be obtained from the warden.

The promontory of Drigg was until the 1980s Europe's largest nesting resort of black headed gulls, with about 10,000 birds at its peak. Several species of tern nested on the dunes but the ternery had gone by 1977. The dunes, which are especially attractive in spring, when acres of sea pinks [thrift] are found, have a sprinkling of birds, including ringed plover and oystercatcher. The resident greylags have their number augmented in winter by immigrant birds. Drigg is a haunt of adders.

Duddon Sands and Dunnerdale. A good starting point for an exploration of this area is the RSPB reserve of Hodbarrow, a short distance from the small Victorian town of Millom. A parking area at Haverigg is within easy walking distance of Hodbarrow Lagoon. Ironstone was mined hereabouts until the workings became flooded. Notice the remains of an old sea wall, grotesquely tilted. A large freshwater lagoon is attractive to bird life being a breeding place of Sandwich, Arctic, common and little terns. If a visit takes place in winter, look out for raptors – peregrine and merlin - preying on the massed birds. Wildfowl and waders on passage are seen at Hodbarrow and there is a moulting flock of red-breasted merganser.

The channels flowing for several miles across the estuary of the River Duddon are flanked on the inner area by sand and saltmarsh.

General views of the estuary are available from Sandside or Foxfield (where there are railway stations). The marshes attract wintering "grey" geese, both greylag and pink-footed, as well as waterfowl – wigeon, teal and pintail. Wading birds not only throng the tideline when the water is ebbing but roost in areas that are not overrun by the tide. Look out for oystercatcher, curlew, dunlin and redshank. The outer estuary is notable for its large sand dunes with some wet areas attractive to birds.

Dunnerdale, also known as the Duddon Valley, is entered with a right turn just before the County Bridge, where there are traffic lights. On the way up the valley, stop near Birks Bridge (single span structure, crossing a deep gorge, the sides of which are bedecked by rowan). The dalehead is bleak, except where Dunnerdale Forest (coniferous) was established. Over 50 species of birds have been known to breed here and the list takes in buzzard, sparrow hawk, kestrel, jay, long and short-eared owls, great and lesser spotted woodpeckers, turtle dove, redstart, kestrel, pied and spotted flycatchers and wood warbler.

At the dalehead, you might (if you feel daring) drive over the Hardknott Pass to Eskdale or continue over the not-quite-so-severe Wrynose Pass into Little Langdale. The austere landscape has a bird population that includes the raven, whinchat and stonechat, ring ouzel, curlew, yellow and grey wagtails. Years ago, springtime dawns were marked by the roo-cooing of black grouse at the lek. This species has suffered a considerable decline.

Eden Valley. The Eden flows northwards from a source near Hell Gill to Solway Firth. Narrow at the dalehead (known as Mallerstang), the valley opens out, fan-like, and the conditions moderate, the land growing arable crops. Oilseed rape, when flowering, enlivens the vale with yellow patches. The buildings are mainly of the attractive New Red Sandstone.

Appleby, the old county town of Westmorland, is a good focal point. As mentioned in the section on geese, the area known as Watersmeet, where the Eamont flows into the Eden, is famous for its wintering wildfowl and may be scanned through binoculars from the roadside between Langwathby and Culgaith. Most commonly the geese are greylag but white-fronted, barnacle and bean geese have also been reported.

Waterfowl such as goldeneye and goosander make every winter-walk along riverside footpaths exciting birding expeditions. Park the car at Langwathby, cross the metal bridge over the Eden and take a right turn to follow a bank of the Eden for a mile or so. Or take the Nunnery Walk (small charge), beginning at a point just north of Kirkoswald.

The usual riverside nesting birds – dipper, grey wagtail, common sandpiper – will be found. Sand martins colonise sandy banks that have now been over-run by Himalayan balsam. Elsewhere, oyster-catchers make use of the extensive shingle beds or adjacent fields.

Woodland in Edenvale holds breeding pairs of redstart, pied fly-catcher, wood warbler and siskin. The crossbill has also been reported. It is not an easy bird to locate, for it nests early and is inclined to stay in the tree-tops, where it dines on seeds of cones. Now that oilseed rape is grown on a considerable scale, enormous flocks of finches – including brambling and linnet - are to be seen during the harvest season. They are preyed on by raptors such as peregrine and merlin.

The East Fellside marks the edge of the northern Pennines. Cross Fell, the highest in a range that extends from Derbyshire into Scotland, presides over the local scene and is traversed by the Pennine Way, the second longest footpath in Britain, being some 250 miles. The Pennine gills are notable for the big crag-nesting birds – peregrine, raven, buzzard – and also for ring ouzels, dippers and grey wagtails.

Elterwater. A shallow, tree-fringed lake between Ambleside and Chapel Stile, in Great Langdale. The name of the lake is said to relate to wild swans, these being whoopers of Iceland origin. A series of reed-reed-edged pools are attractive to water-fowl.

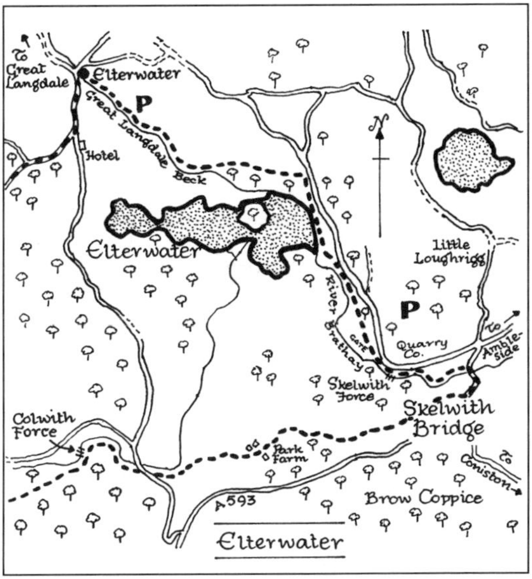

Esthwaite Water.

Situated in Beatrix Potter Country, between Hawkshead and Near Sawrey, this shallow, food-rich lake is edged at the north end by reed swamp and carr, the nesting place of great-crested and little grebes, also greylag. The lake outflows into the south basin of Windermere. A good parking place is situated on the south-western side of the lake, beside the main Newby Bridge-Hawkshead road. (Esthwaite Water has become a notable trout fishery. Fly-fishing only in the north basin, 200 acres. The south basin remains open for bait, lure and fly).

Geltsdale. A reserve of the RSPB on the northern Pennines, south-east of Brampton, on the Carlisle-Newcastle road. You might initially park at Talkin Tarn (Cumbria County Council), a breeding place of tufted duck, common sandpaper and grey wagtail and a large lake where, in the off-season, local bird-watchers approach with a Mikawber attitude. Something interesting is sure to turn up!

The final approach to Geltsdale is on foot from Jockey Shield, east of

Castle Carrock or from Low Gelt Bridge, which will be located east of the A69. Geltsdale is a valley in a tract of expansive moorland holding a good stock of grouse and waders – golden plover, curlew, redshank, snipe – also raven, short-eared owl and ring ouzel. The peregrine and merlin cull smaller birds. The twite, now quite a rare bird, nests in this area. In spring, when the pink-footed geese are heading for their Icelandic nesting ground, you might see lines and chevrons of these grey-geese in transit.

Grasmere and Rydal Water. The heart of Wordsworthshire. (William Wordsworth, a poet with a good knowledge of wild birds, rented property in Grasmere before going to a large rented house in Rydal). In the holiday season, car parking at Grasmere is quickly used up and a good place to park is at one of the tree-shielded parking places at White Moss, just off the main road between the two villages. It is a short walk into Grasmere, thence to Rydal along a fellside path known as Loughrigg Terrace, returning to White Moss by path under Nab Scar.

White Moss Common is served by a nature walk which takes in both woodland and waterside birds – tree-creeper, pied flycatcher, grey wagtail, dipper. Coot, black-headed gulls and a variety of waterfowl are to be seen in winter. Both Canada geese and greylags inhabit the area.

Grizedale Forest (c8,000 acres/3240 hectares). A Forestry Commission holding between Coniston and Esthwaite Water. The main approach is from just south of Hawkshead, where a sporty hill road leads to Grisedale and Satterthwaite. The offices and a Forest Centre, in which forest life is interpreted by imaginative displays, are to be found about two miles from Hawkshead.

The forest is now an interesting blend of coniferous forest (mainly on the high ground) and broad-leaved woodland (the valley sides). The Forestry Commission have long been concerned about wildlife conservation. Several nature trails of short duration may be followed (details from the Forest Centre). The Silurian Way, named after the underlying rock, is a demanding $9^{1}/_{2}$ mile/15.2 km walk. Grizedale Beck runs through a mainly open area.

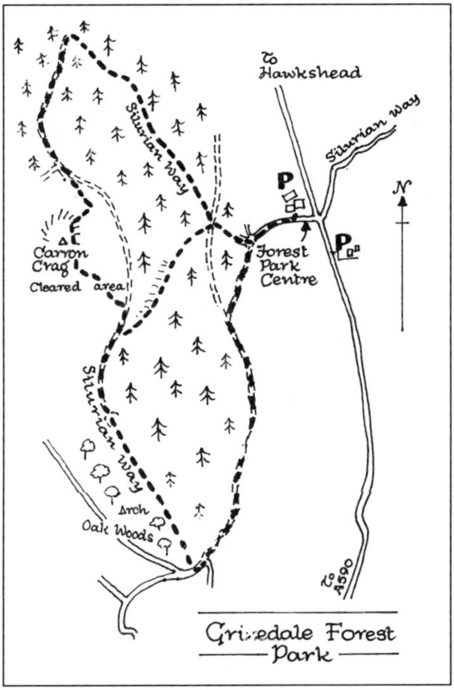

Woodland birds include buzzard, sparrowhawk, several species of owls, nuthatch and, among the "little brown jobs," wood warbler and chiffchaff. The shy hawfinch has been seen, though looking for this tree-top bird usually induces neck-ache. The coniferous area is the nesting place for crossbill, siskin and redpoll. Oakwoods sustain a population of woodpeckers, also two other species which need old timber for nesting, these being redstart and pied flycatcher. Among the titmice, look out for coal and marsh tits. (Field recognition should concentrate on the head patterning. The coal tit, smallest of the family, has a black cap and white cheeks; the marsh tit has a black cap and black bib).

At dusk, during the nesting season, one might see (and hear) roding woodcock. The Commission created ponds for the benefit of waterfowl. As noted elsewhere, there was once an attempt to introduce the capercaillie, the largest grouse in the world, to Grizedale. This praiseworthy venture came to nought.

Haweswater and Wet Sleddale. The RSPB wardens the Haweswater area, which is approached from either Shap or Askham, the long road beside the reservoir being a cul de sac. A small car park will be found where the surfaced road ends. A footpath leads round the top of the lake and into Riggindale. The Coast to Coast Walk devised by A Wainwright runs along the western side of the lake. A sign indicating Wet Sleddale will be seen by the A6 just south of Shap.

Haweswater (3 miles/4.8 km) came into being when the old valley of Mardale, with its two shallow lakes, was flooded. A horse-shoe of fells at the head of the valley includes High Street (referring to a route used in Roman times; there are no shops!) and Kidsty Pike. The area is now best-known for England's only breeding pair of golden eagles. Fellside birds include ravens, peregrines and ring ouzels.

On the southern side of Haweswater is Naddle, an extensive area of mixed coniferous and deciduous trees but with a goodly area of oak. Here nest buzzard, sparrowhawk, green and great spotted woodpeckers, garden and wood warblers, blackcap, pied and spotted flycatchers and woodcock.

Among the waterside species are greylag and Canada geese, mallard, teal, common sandpiper, red-breasted merganser. A small island near the head of the reservoir holds a small breeding colony of herring and lesser black-backed gulls. The cormorant is also said to nest here. Haweswater has long had a winter roost of black-headed and common gulls.

Wet Sleddale is a delightful, if very wet, little valley. Wading birds like the curlew and snipe, and a small duck, the teal, find the wet meadows near the dam to their liking. The reservoir is used by greylag and Canada geese, also by the goosander. Ravens fly at the dalehead.

Humphrey Head. This 170ft/52m headland, one of the highspots of a generally low-lying coastline, is approached by road from Allithwaite (after negotiating a level crossing near Wraysholme, turn left). The headland, which is the last flourish of one of several limestone ridges lying north of the sands of Morecambe Bay, is in part a nature reserve leased by Cumbria Wildlife Trust from Holker Estates. There is a prominent information board at the entry to the reserve. Greylag geese are a winter attraction on the salt marshes flanking the headland. Despite its modest elevation, Humphrey Head is a splendid viewpoint for coastal bird life, especially in winter, when on marsh and mudflat there are numerous oystercatchers, dunlin, shelduck and pintail ducks. (The woodland on the reserve is a resort of red squirrels).

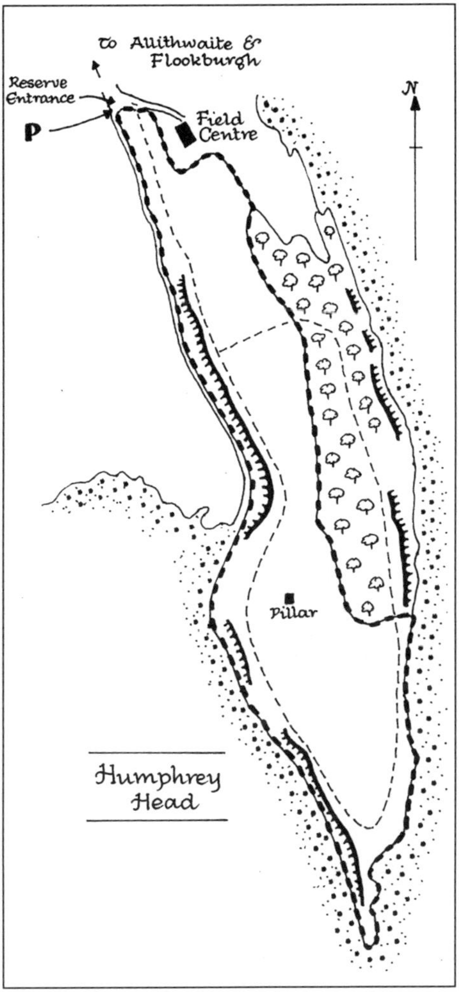

Kent Valley. The River Kent, which has its source at the head of Kentmere and loses its identity in an estuary not many miles away, is reputedly the fastest-flowing river in the land. The river has an infusion of cold water from the River Mint and flows through the old grey town of Kendal. The channel is compressed by limestone outcrops at Low Sizergh.

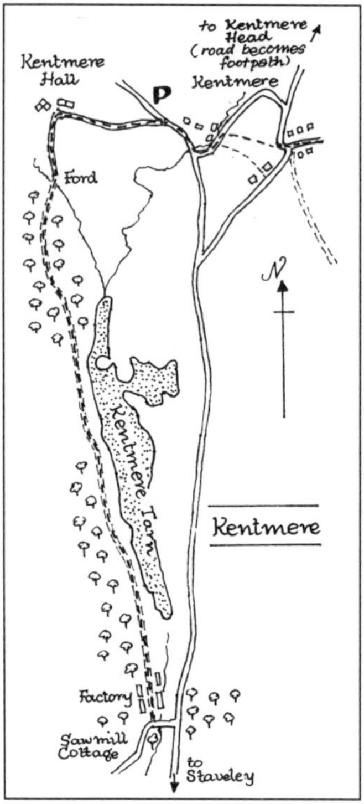

River birds include sand martin and common sandpiper, dipper and grey wagtail. Two comparatively recent arrivals are red-breasted merganser and goosander. The long low form of the cormorant is to be seen. Woodland and scrub beside the Kent are the resort in summer of sedge warbler, garden warbler, chiff chaff and whitethroat. Grey geese follow the line of the Kent valley when commuting across Lakeland. The estuary of the Kent is very watchable. Meathop Marsh has long been a winter resort of migrant greylags, which also spend some of their time in the valley of the Lune.

Killington Reservoir. A good general view of a stretch of water brought into being to top up a local canal is possible from the busy Killington Service area on the southbound carriageway of the M6. A backdrop is provided by the Howgill Fells. Killington (600ft/180m) is a resort of anglers and sailing enthusiasts. There is, nonetheless, a varied bird life. By local agreement, the north bay and a wooded island are kept clear of sportsmen. The island holds a black-headed gullery and is also used by nesting Canada geese. The great-crested grebe is among the visitors. Upland waders like curlew and redshank nest in the area. The list of waterfowl in winter includes wigeon, pochard and tufted duck.

Leighton Moss (321 acres/130 hectares). This famous reserve of the RSPB in North Lancashire lies in a wooded valley between Silverdale and Yealand Redmayne. Reach it handily from Carnforth or Arnside. The reserve is signposted near Silverdale railway station. Adequate car parking is available near an interpretive centre.

Leighton Moss, formerly an inlet of Morecambe Bay, was reclaimed as arable land in a wooded valley between Silverdale and Yealand Redmayne. The area was kept dry by pumping but in 1917, when the fuel ran out, fresh water ran in. Leighton Moss has good paths and well-appointed hides overlooking several shallow, bird-busy meres between beds of phragmites, which are inhabited by bittern, bearded tit (which first bred here in 1973), marsh harrier (of much more recent date) and water rail. Reed warblers are abundant and both sedge and grasshopper warblers can usually be seen. Shingle islands are used by nesting oystercatchers, some black-headed gulls and even a few common terns. Herons stalk the shallows.

Ashwoods in the vicinity are the nesting place of nuthatch and the elusive hawfinch. In winter, while the meres remain unfrozen, large numbers of ducks converge on Leighton Moss. By far the largest number is of mallard and teal. Good views from hides may be had of pintail, shoveler, wigeon, tufted duck, golden eye and pochard. Mute swans are present. Sometimes their wilder cousins, the whoopers and Bewick's, call to rest and refuel.

Inquire at the visitor centre about the RSPB holdings on Carnforth Marsh, where two hides have been set up from which to watch vast numbers of waders at high tide in winter and, in spring, a nesting colony of black-headed gulls.

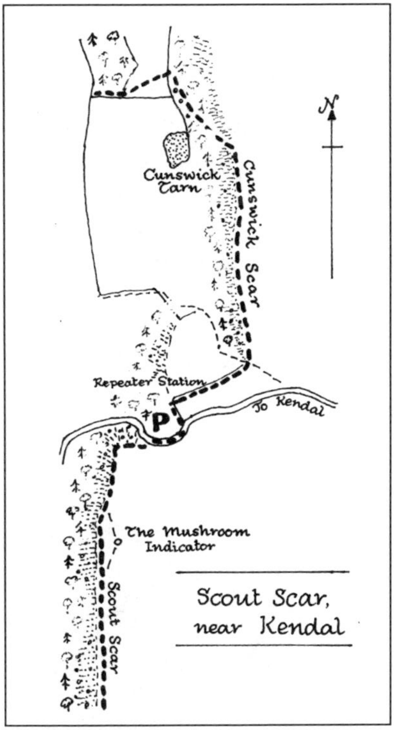

Scout Scar. From Kendal, a road sweeps up grandly to a parking place on a range of limestone scars from which many of the Lakeland peaks might be seen. The long escarpment that takes in Scout Scar and Cunswick Scar is a resort of kestrel and raven. In an area where ants are numerous, a green woodpecker might be seen feeding on the ground. Skylarks fill the air with song during spring and summers. In autumn, thorn berries attract flocks of Scandinavian thrushes (fieldfares with some redwings).

Sizergh Castle (National Trust). Shortly after leaving the Kendal by-pass on the A590 you will see a signpost (pointing right) for Sizergh. In the estate generally, there is access to footpaths and local birds include buzzard, sparrowhawk, curlew, green woodpecker, grey wagtail and redstart. In the grounds of Sizergh Castle, look out in particular for the hawfinch.

St Bees Head. On the Cumbrian coast, to the north of the village of St Bees and just south of Whitehaven. A footpath (the initial leg of the celebrated Coast to Coast route devised by A Wainwright) extends along the cliffs. Alternately, park the car at Sandwith village and follow a private road of about 2 miles/3.2 km to the lighthouse. The headland, of glowing red sandstone, is a celebrated seabird-breeding haunt, with an estimated 5,000 birds in residence during the spring

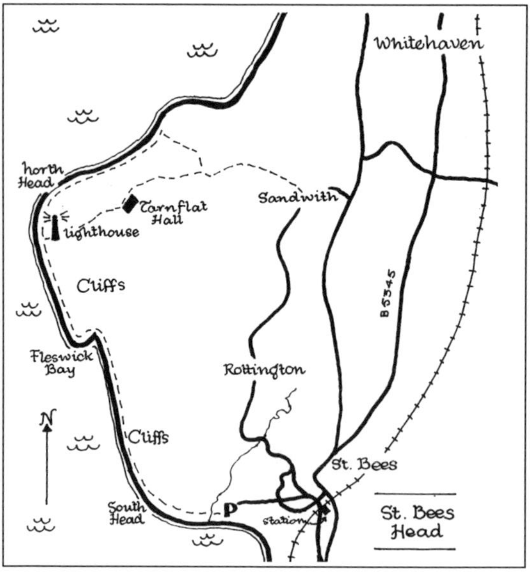

and early summer. St Bees is divided into a North Head and South Head, with Fleswick Bay as the half-way feature. (Here you might see rock pipits). At the highest point, the North Head, is a stubby lighthouse.

St Bees has a goodly number of auks, especially guillemot and razorbill, with a few pairs of puffins and black guillemots. Kittiwakes and fulmars are also among the cliff nesters, with several thousand pairs of herring and lesser black-backed gulls on broad cliff ledges. The raven may be seen. The chough once bred here but is now just an occasional visitor from its Manx haunts.

Watching migrating seabirds is an increasingly popular occupation. You need powerful binoculars and durable waterproof clothing. At migration times, birds to be seen from St Bees include divers, grebes, terns, skuas, also (in midsummer) Manx shearwater and gannet. In autumn, the passage of both Leach's and storm petrels has been recorded. Nearer to hand is the springtime movement northwards of birds including chats and warblers.

Sunbiggin Tarn. A high-level (1,000ft/300m) moorland tarn near the village of Orton. The tarn lies in a basin of undulating moorland in what is predominantly limestone country known to those who are walking the Coast to Coast route from St Bees to Robin Hood's Bay. An outlet stream joins Rais Beck, which flows into the Lune at Gaisgill. The area of open water at Sunbiggin normally amounts to about 10 acres/4 hectares for the main pond. A treacherous reed and sedge swamp lies between the Tarn and a shallow area of water known as Cow Dub.

Sunbiggin has an all-the-year-round appeal for bird-watchers, though when frozen its appeal to waterfowl is limited. The winter visitors include whooper swan and a variety of duck, also red-breasted merganser, goosander and – cormorant! Winter is a time to see foraging ravens and several birds of prey. Life at the Tarn is at its rowdiest in spring when a large black-headed gullery is established, the birds giving their raucous calls at all times of day and night. Nesting on the moors round about are curlew and dunlin.

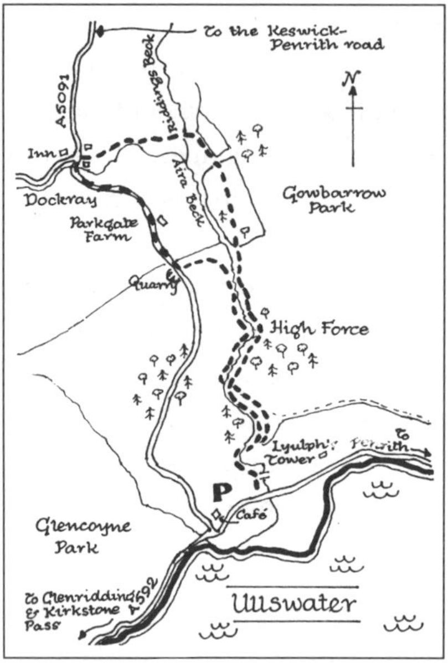

Ullswater. The second largest lake in the region (8 miles/13 km). On the map, Ullswater resembles a dog's leg, with two bends. Around the head of the lake, fells seem to spring out of the water like mountains from fjords. At Pooley Bridge, where Ullswater overflows, the landscape is pastoral. Breeding water birds include red-breasted merganser, coot, redshank, common sandpiper, dipper and grey wagtail. In winter, the lake has a gull roost, with up to 25,000 birds, mainly common and black-headed but with small numbers of the larger gulls, such as great black-backed. Winter wildfowl include cormorant, greylag, whooper swan, wigeon, pochard, tufted duck, goldeneye and goosander. Also occasionally seen: common scoter, scaup and long-tailed duck.

On the western side of Ullswater are splendid oakwoods (Glencoyne, Gowbarrow, Sandwick). Here you might see buzzard, sparrowhawk, tawny owl, various woodpeckers, nuthatch, redstart, pied flycatcher, wood warbler, siskin and redpoll. Visit Aira Force (see map).

South Walney. A reserve administered by the Cumbrian Wildlife Trust. Walney island is now tethered to the mainland at Barrow-in-Furness by a substantial bridge. A stranger with romantic ideas about islands is initially a little dismayed to enter a Victorian and Edwardian suburb of Barrow. Turn south, passing the quaint little village of Biggar for a road beside the sea (and a refuse dump, the resort of many scavenging gulls). On the reserve itself are sand dunes, areas of shingle, freshwater lagoons – and birds by the thousand. Sea views take in eiders, shelduck and (in winter) hosts of waders.

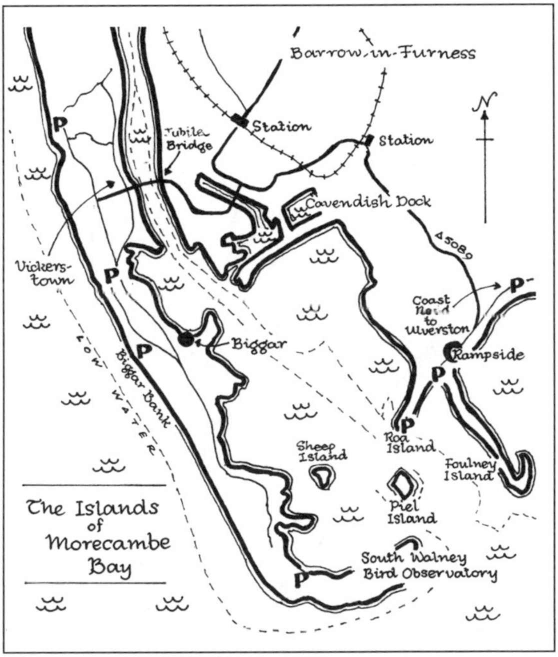

Dotted lines indicate low water

Here is the southernmost breeding site for eiders on the west coast of Britain. South Walney is also the nesting ground of almost a quarter of the world's population of lesser black-backed gulls. Intermixed are a vast number of nesting pairs of herring gulls. There is a ternery on a spit of land near the lighthouse.

August is the best time to see migrant birds heading south to winter quarters in Africa. The author once observed a hoopoe on South Walney. In rough weather, sea-watchers from a hide see oceanic birds – gannet, Manx shearwater, Arctic skua – in transit.

Whitbarrow. The "white" hill, which has a maximum height of 707ft/215m, dominates the eastern end of the A590. Use a minor turn-off for Millside and park the car beside the former highway before

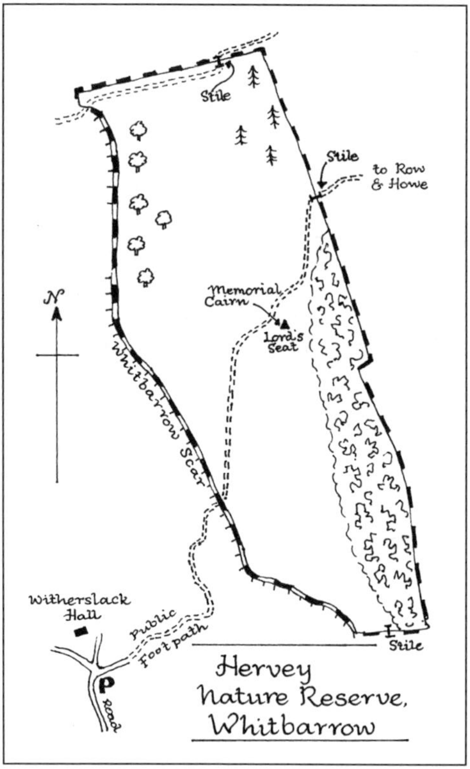

setting off on the short walk to the hill, via the village, bearing right towards Buckstone Wood and using a zig-zag path through bird-busy woodland to the hilltop. Though mainly noted for its diverse plant life, and local deer (red and roe), Whitbarrow and its adjacent woodland has a good variety of bird life.

Windermere. ($10^{1}/_{2}$ miles/17 km). The head of the lake is set against a backdrop of volcanic fells. On either side of Windermere are more gentle Silurian hills, with woodland and lots of tarns. A car-ferry operates between a point south of Bowness and one near Ferry House, headquarters of the Freshwater Biological Association. Visit the National Park Centre just north of the town of Windermere (so named after the lake when the railway arrived in the first part of the 19th century).

There might be 1,000 boats on Windermere on a bright summer's day, but birds do manage to find nesting places and Bowness Bay, which is near a group of wooded islands, is thronged by birds as well as day-trippers, these birds being scavenging ducks and swans. The ducks are nominally mallard but in some cases hybridisation has occurred with domestic strains.

Windermere comes into its own when its quiet bays, especially those on the western shoreline, are used by wintering waterfowl. Reed-beds are the summer resort of reed bunting and sedge warbler. Listen also for the cheery call of common sandpiper. Look for diving duck, including wintering goldeneye, at Waterhead, Fell Foot or in the lee of the islands, where they are in close view of those using the ferryboat. Among the more unusual birds seen are scaup, smew and scoter.

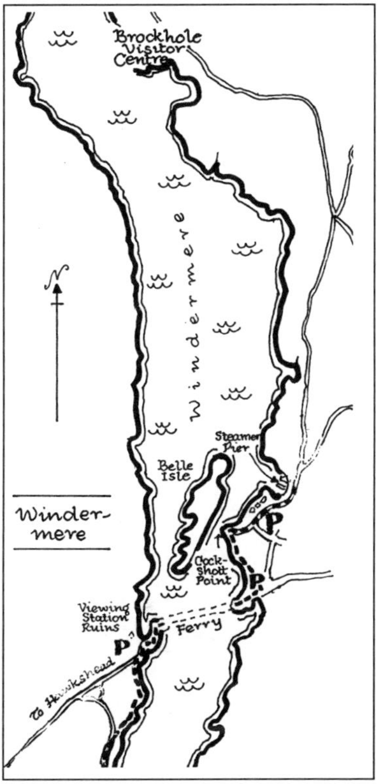

In winter, quite large numbers of cormorants frequent Windermere. This and adjacent lakes have a feral population of greylags. A flight-line high above Windermere is used by pinkfooted geese travelling between the estuary of the Ribble and Solway Firth. Wintering gulls roost between Belle Island and Millerground.

A Personal Check List

This list is not exhaustive, so space is left at the end for birds not listed.

NAME	WHERE SEEN	DATE
Great Crested Grebe 95		
Little Grebe		
Fulmar		
Cormorant 89		
Bittern 24		
Grey Heron 91		
Mute Swan 86		
Whooper Swan 86		
Bewick's Swan 86		
Greylag Goose 88		
Pink-footed Goose 102		
Barnacle Goose		
Canada Goose		
Shelduck 104		

NAME	WHERE SEEN	DATE
Mallard		
Wigeon		
Pintail		
Shoveler 92		
Teal		
Pochard		
Tufted Duck 95 (23)		
Eider 105		
Long-tailed Duck		
Goldeneye 95		
Red-breasted Merganser 96		
Goosander 97		
Golden Eagle 47		
Buzzard 71		
Red Kite		
Goshawk		
Sparrowhawk 75		
Marsh Harrier		
Kestrel 61		

NAME		WHERE SEEN	DATE
Merlin	56		
Peregrine	49		
Red Grouse	57		
Black Grouse	57		
Pheasant	77		
Grey Partridge			
Water Rail			
Moorhen			
Coot	94		
Oystercatcher	102		
Ringed Plover			
Dotterel	48		
Golden Plover	59		
Lapwing	66		
Knot			
Sanderling			
Dunlin			
Purple Sandpiper			
Snipe			
BITTERN	24		

NAME	WHERE SEEN	DATE
Woodcock 76		
Curlew 65		
Whimbrel		
Bar-tailed Godwit		
Redshank 107		
Greenshank		
Common Sandpiper 90		
Kittiwake		
Black-headed Gull		
Common Gull		
Great Black-backed Gull		
Lesser Black-backed Gull		
Herring Gull		
Artic Tern		
Common Tern		
Sandwich Tern		
Guillemot		
Black Guillemot		
Puffin		

NAME	WHERE SEEN	DATE
Collared Dove		
Cuckoo		
Rock Dove		
Stock Dove		
Woodpigeon		
Barn Owl 62		
Little Owl		
Long-eared Owl		
Short-eared Owl		
TAWNY OWL 73		
Nightjar		
Kingfisher 89		
Green Woodpecker 78		
Great Spotted Woodpecker 79		
Lesser Spotted Woodpecker		
Skylark 51		
Swift		
Sand Martin 91		
Swallow 64		
House Martin		

NAME		WHERE SEEN	DATE
Meadow Pipit	56		
Rock Pipit			
Yellow Wagtail			
Grey Wagtail	79		
Pied Wagtail			
Waxwing			
Dipper	97		
Wren	52		
Hedge Sparrow			
Robin			
Redstart	81		
Whinchat	84		
Stonechat			
Wheatear	54		
Ring Ouzel	53		
Blackbird			
Redwing			
Fieldfare	67	7	
Song Thrush			
GOLDCREST	41		

NAME	WHERE SEEN	DATE
Mistle Thrush		
Reed Warbler		
Marsh Warbler		
Sedge Warbler		
Whitethroat		
Garden Warbler 83		
Blackcap		
Wood Warbler 83		
Chiffchaff		
Willow Warbler 83		
Goldcrest 74 (41)		
Spotted Flycatcher		
Pied Flycatcher 80		
Bearded Tit		
Long-tailed Tit		
Blue Tit		
Great Tit		
Marsh Tit		
Coal Tit		

NAME		WHERE SEEN	DATE
Nuthatch	78		
Treecreeper	82		
Jay	73		
Chough			
Jackdaw	61		
Rook			
Carrion Crow	60		
Raven	43		
Starling			
House Sparrow			
Chaffinch	81		
Brambling			
Garden Warbler			
Bullfinch			
Hawfinch			
Goldfinch	68		
Greenfinch			
Siskin			
Linnet			

NAME	WHERE SEEN	DATE
Twite		
Redpoll		
Crossbill 84		
Snow Bunting 53 (23)		
Reed Bunting		
Yellow Hammer		

Redwings

Other species seen –

NAME	WHERE SEEN	DATE

If you have enjoyed the artwork in this book,
you will enjoy a visit to

Brent Gallery, Cowling

where a range of drawings and paintings
by David Binns is on permanent display

Educated in Skipton and at Leeds College of Arts, where he obtained the National Diploma in Design (Illustration), his teaching career eventually took him back to his old school, Ermysted's Grammar School in Skipton as head of the art department. Subsequently, David spent a dozen years with his family as a freelance artist living in Northumberland, overlooking the famous Lindisfarne Nature Reserve. Here, with his wife Molly, he established the Brent Gallery, named after the geese that wintered on the reserve.

David was elected to the Society of Wildlife Artists in 1968 and has regularly exhibited at their annual exhibition in the Mall Galleries, London. At these exhibitions he has won the RSPB Fine Art Award a record four times. Now he lives back in Yorkshire, the birds and animals found against the Pennine dales and fells return as subjects for his widely published work and watercolours.

Brent Gallery, 60a Keighley Road, Cowling, West Yorkshire
Tel. 01535 636892

Whooper Swans